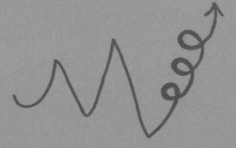

*TO KILL A MOCKINGBIRD* BY HARPER LEE

*HOPSCOTCH* BY JULIO CORTÁZAR

Juan Rodrigo Llaguno

**Martín Solares** is the author of the novels *Don't Send Flowers* and *The Black Minutes*, which was a finalist for France's most prestigious award for crime fiction, the Grand Prix de Littérature Policière, and for the distinguished Spanish-language award, the Rómulo Gallegos Prize. He lives in Mexico City.

# HOW TO DRAW A NOVEL

Also by Martín Solares

*The Black Minutes*

*Don't Send Flowers*

# HOW TO DRAW A NOVEL

# MARTÍN SOLARES

Translated from the Spanish
by Heather Cleary

Grove Press
*New York*

FIRST EDITION

*Published simultaneously in Canada*
*Printed in the United States of America*

Martín Solares is represented by Schavelzon Graham Agencia
Literaria, schavelzongraham.com.

Originally published in the Spanish language as *Como dibujar una
novela* in 2014 by Ediciones Era.

First Grove Atlantic publication, including material added for this
edition: December 2023

Library of Congress Cataloging-in-Publication data is available for this
title.

ISBN 978-0-8021-5930-4
eISBN 978-0-8021-5931-1

Grove Press
an imprint of Grove Atlantic
154 West 14th Street
New York, NY 10011

Distributed by Publishers Group West

groveatlantic.com

23 24 25 26   10 9 8 7 6 5 4 3 2 1

# Inventory

# HOW TO DRAW A NOVEL

# The Welcome Mat

This book is a collection of drawings and notes about novels, those strange beings that live among us. Generations have lifted their eyes to them: for some, they are constellations made of words; for others, they are like a powerful spell. From their very first phrase, they transport us to a place where words hold more than one meaning and the laws of physics do not apply. Baptized by their authors with evocative, enigmatic names that are sometimes the first words of that spell, they are often baptized a second time by readers wanting to make them more familiar, bring them closer.

Life forces us to choose between what's behind door number one and what's behind door number two, however captivating each option might be, but a well-constructed novel can open several doors at once, offering us scenes that are surprising or impassioned, unsettling or amusing: monumental failures, ambitious endeavors, and seemingly impossible achievements.

They don't tell us how to live, exactly—they tell us stories. When times are tough, in those moments when we search for ways to overcome life's worries, novels offer us tales that seem to have been written as a commentary on our situation.

Built to surprise, they are now also expected to be beautiful. And they know a thing or two about life: when they are well constructed, they even seem to think. Instead of presenting argument, thesis, antithesis, and synthesis, the novel offers setting, conflict, and characters—through these, we understand something about how the world works.

On the basis of the conviction that novels think, this book will explore some of their most fascinating traits: what strategies writers use in designing the opening lines of their stories, how a character is born, how fast the prose moves, how everyday objects behave in the world of fiction, what images novelists have created to describe novels, and a few short texts about how these stories often end. One chapter of this book asks if certain novels might leave us with the sensation that we can see or even inhabit a building made of words that begs to be visited and enjoyed in detail, like an extraordinary dream.

Anyone who has tried to sketch the shape of a dream will agree that the material is difficult to capture. Seen from above, the drawing of a dream often looks like a spiral or an eddy, with its ends disappearing in the distance:

This shape evokes the line of a short story, whereas novels tend to be more spread out:

The short story is vertical prose that tends to round itself out; the novel is horizontal prose that crests each time we ask what will happen next.

Like a dream, a short story blasts off, surprises us, and ends. A novel, on the other hand, like a waking dream, is a journey we'll never forget.

Spinal column of a novel discovered in
Tampico, circa 1996

# Doubles Cast in Shades
# of Night

At first, they are faceless shadows, beings of smoke and mirrors we never manage to see clearly: doubles that emerge from the night of our lives, as Bakhtin describes them. With the exception of those miraculous cases when everything just falls into place, they are usually discovered gradually by constructing, shaping, or inserting their defining characteristics.

We appreciate their relative malleability as we work on them, as long as we're making the story more, rather than less, coherent. We have a lump of red playdough in our hands. The lump swells, it expands upward and downward and after growing in all directions, it begins to take shape. Like each element in the novel, a character is a bit like a sculpture, a concentration of energy and time.

Some can accomplish this with a single stroke of the pen. Julio Ramón Ribeyro, for example, could create a disturbing character in under three sentences:

The surprise or rather the terror produced in me by the Agency employee with the atrophied arm, that arm which was shorter than the other and ended in a hand which was not a hand but rather a kind of stump with fingernails, was also felt by the waiter. In that moment, I realized that the limb I had viewed as a weakness, and for which I pitied the man, was in fact his habitual instrument of aggression.

*Prosas apátridas* (Stateless writings)

Sometimes, characters come from details gathered at the most unexpected moments. I'd bet money that Julio Cortázar baptized Rocamadour, La Maga's baby in *Hopscotch*, after tasting a soft, delicately flavored cheese that can be found in Paris.

Great characters rarely show up alone. As soon as we catch sight of one, we discover a whole pack on their heels—attacking them, testing them, revealing different aspects of their nature. Fernando Savater has said that a hero needs two things: a loyal friend and a tireless enemy.

A great character is a constellation, the magnetic center of its own solar system. If they are well constructed, great characters produce two kinds of magnetism: on one hand, they attract other beings, loyal or adversarial, to enrich the story; on the other, they also excite and move the reader with their responses to the challenges that face them. Though they are beings without viscera, as Paul Valéry has said, we are captivated by fictional characters because they dare to tread where we never would: they murder the old prostitute, betray friends in need, steal from their own mothers, rush to confront a killer, abandon a faithful and devoted lover in their moment of greatest need. They are the guinea pigs in the laboratory of the novel, experimental egos that cross boundaries on our behalf. They differ from us in that they are able to muster courage, fortitude, and resolve on a scale that few people could hope to match. This is why they must be chosen carefully: they are of central importance to the experiment. Hercule Poirot and his egg-shaped head, Sherlock Holmes and his hobby of playing the violin, Maigret and the sandwiches he orders from the restaurant on the corner, Philip Marlowe and his gimlet, Inspector Wallander and his struggles with the practical details of his life . . . Notable eccentricities and unusual hobbies abound.

And yet characters are more than just a list of characteristics. They are not made through mere accumulation, but rather through careful selection. It only takes a few well-chosen traits—contradictory ones, whenever possible—and we begin to imagine them as perfect, fully developed beings. Rudyard Kipling's characters always have an occupation and a flaw: Kim is a messenger who is scared of snakes (even though snakes are a symbol of Mercury and of the most accomplished messengers); Mahbub Ali is a horse trader who rejects all things spiritual; the conjurer seems omnipotent but is vulnerable to poison; and the ascetic lama offers opinions about life on earth but has no physical or sensual life whatsoever, and believes anything that can be touched can breed sin.

Tabucchi needed just one attribute to create unforgettable beings that shed light on his protagonist's soul with their mere presence. What's Pereira's fan like? Asthmatic. Why do we notice the woman he sees on the train? Because she has a prosthetic leg. What do we remember about Marta, Monteiro Rossi's girlfriend? The crossed straps of her dress. For the Italian writer, the blank page is a glass of water into which a few drops of paint are allowed to fall. In the reader's mind, these drops mix together and enrich one another. We know that the building's caretaker is cooperating with the dictatorship because she reeks of fried food, and she reeks of fried food because she is cooperating with the dictatorship. To uncover these traits, we must pay close attention to where the shadows fall.

One way of listening to a character and getting to the bottom of their essential characteristics, according to the famous script consultant Linda Seger, is to ask what they want, and why they believe what they want is good: not even the worst people in the world see themselves as bad, the screenwriter argues; they believe they are working toward a positive end.

We can listen to fictional characters, but it's also important to see them. Balzac imagined them as little animals, and even kept an animal figurine on his desk for each of the main characters in his novels.

In his writings on the aesthetics of literary creation in *Estética de la creación verbal* (The aesthetics of verbal art), Mikhail Bakhtin suggests that in order to attract great characters, authors should step back from, or even completely out of, their work. The thing is, we fiction writers tend to talk about ourselves, and our characters end up being an often-predictable reflection of our own biographies. If we want interesting characters to appear, first we have to understand them: see them through the eyes of the imaginary beings that surround them, find out what those beings think of them, explore the world in which they operate and ask what will happen after their death, which will always result from the sum total of their actions.

According to Alejandro Jodorowsky, coming up with an unforgettable character is like solving a math problem. In *The Dance of Reality*, he says that when he was coming up with characters like Detective Cabeza de Perro and Prince Manco he made conscious use of the four basic operations: addition, subtraction, multiplication, and division—techniques frequently employed in writing and film. "With addition, which is equivalent to enlargement, I considered how literature and cinema have used this technique to exhaustion. An ape becomes King Kong, a lizard becomes Godzilla, or an insect becomes Mothra, a butterfly so enormous that the movement of its wings brings about hurricanes. This explains the existence of Lilliputians and gnomes in fairy tales; that Bruegel painted the invasion of a thousand skeletons; and the Bible, a plague of locusts. Jodorowsky also suggests making monsters through implantation and metamorphosis, so that "the hands of an assassin are detached from his dead body and grafted onto a pianist who has lost those precious appendages in an accident; they then acquire their own will and force the musician to commit murder." Or making the abstract concrete. "Betrayal: a skinless person who jumps into another's skin." To prove this method works, Jodorowsky needs to cite just one example, which stands alone as a microfiction: "My mother grabbed me, first with two arms, then six, and finally eight arms: now she was a tarantula."

There comes a moment when the author of a novel realizes that they have in front of them a group of beings that govern the plot. All that remains is to follow this fascinating universe and, if the story stalls, run a diagnostic. Check to see if one of them is holding the others in the state they were in when the story began, whether that character might be keeping them from a major transformation.

With characters, as with cars, it's all too easy to copy a model someone has already made without realizing it. So it's not a bad idea to examine the form our creations take. Our characters should ask themselves: "Am I the same old vehicle, the hero of so many bad detective novels, the one who always sounds the same whether I'm in London or Turkey—the predictable, conventional vigilante who always catches the criminal and conquers the most beautiful women, the one who brags about his exploits with exaggerated irony? Am I a cliché, or am I the selfless Lew Archer, the understanding Maigret, the irritable Costas Haritos, the implacable Agent Guedes in Rio de Janeiro or Lituma in the Andes, the conquering Paolo Mandrake, the curious Sherlock Holmes, the spellbinding Auguste Dupin, the anonymous agent from the Continental, the quixotic Philip Marlowe—who specializes in having the last word, even when his teeth are being knocked out—or the obstinate Sam Spade, who won't rest until he solves his partner's murder? If I'm a character in the making, did they design me to go 120 miles per hour so the reader doesn't notice the inconsistencies in the plot, or—on the contrary—am I made to plow slowly through a corrupt society as I evoke a few of life's pleasures and meet other beings who deserve to outlive their author? Ultimately, when we copy another writer's characters, we are stating loud and clear whether we have our own ideas or are happy enough to repeat someone else's. Some writers are perfectly happy in the same old car, but if you're going to get behind the wheel of someone else's ride, first you should take it apart, study it closely, and get rid of the parts you don't need.

Knowing too much about themselves or what awaits them can kill a character. As August Strindberg points out in *Théâtre cruel et théâtre mystique* (Cruel theater and mystical theater), we must remember that protagonists are like horses forced to pass through a massive gorge: "The heroes of a story always wear a blindfold. Otherwise, they would refuse to take a single step and the action would grind to a stop."

It often happens in the process of writing fiction that we invent characters who remind us of someone we know and we try to protect or praise them: this might be the source of the world's most boring stories. If a character who shows up in your work reminds you of a relative or one of the people you love most in the world, kill them or put them in danger immediately. Otherwise, everything you say about them will seem like one long tribute. The novel seeks the unexpected, the unknown, the amusing, and the terrifying.

Another thing: if certain Broadway producers don't hesitate to fire the star of a show one week before opening night, you shouldn't hesitate to get rid of your protagonist if it becomes clear that they are tripping up the plot rather than helping it flow.

Before putting the final touches on a story, Jean-Claude Carrière advises, it's not a bad idea to ask ourselves if we've given each secondary character a moment to shine. Robert McKee, an authority on screenwriting, adds a similar point: have we given each secondary character traits powerful enough that we could convince a great actor to play the role?

Characters are mysterious symbols, even to their authors—a glass that only fills to the brim after the novel is over. Their meaning will never be completely decoded: the author designs the shape of the glass and the reader brings half its contents. This is how characters can continue to grow and develop in the readers' minds over the course of their lives.

There is no question that characters are the motor of the novel. How they come into being and why they last, however, remains a mystery. Why do we still read about Tom Sawyer and his adventures? Why do we want to know the fate of the three musketeers, of Captain Nemo, of Ishmael and Queequeg, Nadja and Breton? Why do we want to be there at the end of this curious game of chess composed of fictional beings who seem to speak about life?

In *Building a Character*, Konstantin Stanislavski describes how he created his first character. After emphasizing that the goal is to construct not a cliché but rather something tangible and three-dimensional, and that this requires instilling and developing the necessary elements in oneself, Stanislavski asserts that when an actor is truly committed to producing a character, they undergo an unexpected change. "One is no longer oneself," he writes. "Or, to be more precise, one is no longer alone in oneself and begins to find the company of that other for whom one had been searching in vain." The first time Stanislavski took an acting class, the professor sent the students down into storage to pick out a costume, from which they would create a character that they would bring to the stage eight days later. Stanislavski recounts that he picked a gray suit. He chose it without thinking, by intuition, but was then completely blocked for the next seven days. He had no idea who the being was that was supposed to wear that suit. For a whole week, all he did was say to himself: You're useless, you'll never make anything worthwhile, you have no talent for acting, you're never going to make it. The day of the final exam arrived, and Stanislavski was still hearing that voice. When the professor instructed them to show their characters, he saw that his classmates were already wearing their costumes and had managed to create fictional beings, no matter how ridiculous. Everyone but him. He was about to give up and walk out when he saw a pot of green cream used to remove stage makeup. He realized that it was exactly what he'd been missing. He covered his face and hands with the cream, put on a top hat, and ran onto the stage, where the exam was already in progress. When the professor saw the late arrival, he shouted, "Who is this who just showed up?" to which Stanislavski replied, "Carry on, don't stop on my account. I'm a critic who came to see the new talent." The professor, who didn't recognize him at first, yelled in a fury that it was a closed rehearsal, that critics weren't allowed in, and then asked the critic who he was. Stanislavski replied, "I'm the critic who lives inside Stanislavski, the one who tells him he does everything wrong." Recognizing his student, the professor played along and went to confront him as if he really were a critic, even threatening to kick him into the street. Just as the man was about to give him a shove, Stanislavski suddenly embraced him, saying, "You can't throw me out. I used to live inside Stanislavski, but now I'm going to live inside you."

Intuitively, and almost as if it were a joke, this great acting coach discovered that characters are born with no small effort from a place deep within us, and that sometimes, if they are well constructed, they live on inside the reader forever.

Maybe this is why we go on reading and writing: because nothing compares to that perfect moment when we discover that other version of us—that freer, more courageous being we call a character.

An overly nebulous novel

# Into the Fog

Let's check the front door with a cold eye to technique.

According to the Book of Genesis, "In the beginning, God created the heavens and the earth." But in the New Testament: "In the beginning was the word." Virgil started out with two nouns and a verb: "I sing of arms and the man." Dante, with a place: "Midway along the journey of our life." Proust, with a circumstance: "For a long time, I went to bed early." *One Thousand and One Nights* and the *Iliad*, with the act of recounting or singing: "It is related (but God alone is all-knowing, as well as all-wise, and almighty, and all-bountiful) that there was, in ancient times, a King of the countries of India and China, possessing numerous troops, and guards, and servants, and domestic dependents: and he had two sons; one of whom was a man of mature age; and the other, a youth" and "Sing, Goddess, Achilles' rage, / Black and murderous, that cost the Greeks / Incalculable pain, pitched countless souls / Of heroes into Hades' dark, / And left their bodies to rot as feasts / For dogs and birds, as Zeus' will was done."

Crossing the threshold of a novel often feels like stepping into a dense fog. Our eyes gradually adjust and we are able to decipher that first cloud. The most important thing is that the reader feels surprised, shaken up, disconcerted by the opening image. That they need to slow down to find an explanation for the mystery. That they realize they've stepped into a world where everything seems more concentrated or more diffuse, where things happen differently. That they ask: Where did this thing I'm reading come from? What language is it written in?

A novel can produce this sense of disorientation long before its first sentence: it can begin with a prologue written by another character, with a particularly intense epigraph, or even with the title itself, if it was chosen for that purpose. Does *Hopscotch* begin with the opening line, "Would I find La Maga?" or with the instructions for reading the book?

According to Jean Verrier, in the Middle Ages texts were thought to begin with their titles. Books were often read out loud by a professional actor, and the plot was announced in the title of each chapter so the public would know, from the start, whether they wanted to keep listening. Only in the Spanish-speaking world have authors maintained this tradition: there are the long, detailed titles at the beginning of each chapter of *Don Quixote*, Sergio Pitol's *Taming the Divine Heron*, and Gabriel García Márquez's *The Story of a Shipwrecked Sailor*. When the first version of this book appeared in a newspaper, the Colombian writer knew he would only have one line to catch the reader's attention, which led to titles like: "How My Shipmates Died at Sea," "My Last Minutes aboard the 'Wolf Ship,'" "Watching Four of My Shipmates Drown," and "My First Night Alone in the Caribbean."

Other contemporary writers aren't too shabby at this, either. The opening chapter of Truman Capote's *In Cold Blood* is called "The Last to See Them Alive." And then there's this one, from Sergio Pitol's *Domar a la divina garza* (Taming the divine heron): "In which an aging novelist, deeply troubled by his years, presents his laboratory and reflects on the material he plans to use for a new novel."

There's also a writer who shows us that the novel can start a little later, with the dedication. Hugo Hiriart has a legendary essay in *Disertación sobre las telarañas* (Dissertation on the cobwebs) in which he laments that this art of beginnings has been completely forgotten. In this dazzling essay, Hiriart invented a series of dedications that have survived the passage of time. Among these: "For don Miguel González Avelar, for the unforgettable night of passion we shared at Madame Backbreaker's," which nearly ended the politician's career, and "For all of humanity, except Enrique Krauze," an homage Krauze reciprocated in a newspaper article a few days later. Among fictional characters, I don't think any has dedicated their fictive memoir with the marksmanship of one of Jorge Ibargüengoitia's inventions, General José Guadalupe Arroyo:

For Matilde, my helpmate of so many years, paragon of Mexican womanhood, who learned to endure with

a smile on her lips the bitter chalice of wedlock with
a man of integrity.

Another minor and rarely used resource—but one no less
capable of jumpstarting a novel—is the foreword. The
declaration at the beginning of Reinaldo Arenas's *Hallucinations* is a statement on the line between fiction and
reality:

> This is the life of Fray Servando Teresa de Mier. Such
> as it was, and could have been; such as I should have
> liked it to have been. It is meant to be simply a novel,
> rather than a biographical or historical novel.

Thomas Bernhard also opens *Wittgenstein's Nephew* with
a delicious clarification that plunges us right away into
the story to come: "Two hundred friends will come to my
funeral and you must make a speech at the graveside."

The important thing is that from the title, the dedication, or the foreword, the reader feels like they are stepping into another time and place, like they are beginning a journey that is going to change their life. Novels transform the reader; to this end, Salvador Elizondo suggests that the book we are reading wasn't even written, but instead is being dreamed by the author and the reader. We see this at the beginning of his extraordinary short novel *Elsinore*:

> I am writing this story in a dream. The images spin around me, chasing one another in a dizzying cyclone. I see myself writing in this notebook as if I were caught inside a parenthesis within the dream, in the eye of a vortex of figures at once familiar and unknown to me that emerge from the fog, appear for an instant, circulate, speak, gesticulate, and then fall as still as photographs before disappearing into the abyss of the night, startled by the avalanche of oblivion, and plunging into the unsettling stillness of the lake. The words I hear as I dream I am writing seem to come from the beyond, from some vigil far removed in space and time, and though I can hear them clearly, I cannot understand them, as if they were being spoken in a vestigial and forgotten tongue.

Beginnings can also take the form of a summary, as in Ernesto Sábato's *The Tunnel*: "It should be sufficient to say that I am Juan Pablo Castel, the painter who killed María Iribarne. I imagine that the trial is still in everyone's mind and that no further information about myself is necessary." Paul Auster achieves them often: "I was looking for a quiet place to die," or "It was the summer that men first walked on the moon," or even "Six days ago, a man blew himself up by the side of a road in northern Wisconsin." In Hemingway's hands, these summaries take on the tone of a modern legend: "He was an old man who fished alone in a skiff in the Gulf Stream and he had gone eighty-four days now without taking a fish."

Sometimes they can focus on a single detail that distills the meaning of the entire opening scene: "The man was so tall and thin he seemed to be always in profile," and "The Sergeant takes a look at Sister Patrocinio and the botfly is still there." We need only to see that botfly to understand that we're dealing with a corpse, a police investigation, a wave of crime rippling through society.

They can also center on an enigmatic image that distills the project of the novel as a whole. Like in Witold Gombrowicz's *Ferdydurke*:

That Tuesday I awoke at the still and empty hour when the night is nearly over but there is still no sign of dawn.

Or, again, in *Hallucinations*:

For many years Fray Servando had been fleeing the Spanish Inquisition all across Europe, constantly beset by the humiliations and hardships that exile and banishment impose, when one afternoon, in a botanical garden in Italy, he came across a thing which brought tears of despair and dejection to his eyes—a Mexican agave, the yucca, or century plant, which is pervasive throughout Mexico. This specimen was jailed in a little cell, behind a protective picket, and it had attached to it a kind of ID card. The friar had been forced to run for a very long time indeed only to come up against this object that identified and reflected him: a cactus, pulled up and transplanted to a foreign land with its foreign sky.

It's strange for a monk to identify with a maguey, but it's not the strangest thing to have happened in the world of fiction. When novels begin with an image, this image often serves as bait:

I would rather not have seen the man, the first time he came into the store, except for his hands: slow, fearful and clumsy, moving without confidence, long and not yet tanned, begging pardon for their dis- interested behavior. He asked a few questions and drank a bottle of beer, standing at the darkest end of the counter, his face turned—past a foreground of sandals, the calendar, sausages turned white by the years—toward the outside, toward the setting sun and the violet crest of the mountains, while waiting

for the bus that would take him to the door of the
old hotel. (Juan Carlos Onetti, *The Goodbyes*)

Freud would say that this first image has a better chance
of capturing the reader's interest if it contains the seed,
or the promise, of some unsettling element that demands
further examination:

> Maman died today. Or yesterday maybe, I don't
> know. (Albert Camus, *The Stranger*)

> Someone must have been telling tales about Josef
> K., for one morning, without having done anything
> wrong, he was arrested. (Franz Kafka, *The Trial*)

Or:

> When Gregor Samsa woke one morning from trou-
> bled dreams, he found himself transformed right
> there in his bed into some sort of monstrous insect.
> (Kafka, *The Metamorphosis*)

Science fiction writers like to offer not just a detail, but
an entire unsettling universe to stir the reader. Have a
look at the beginning of this speculative novel by Richard
Matheson about a world ruled by the living dead:

> On those cloudy days, Robert Neville was never sure
> when sunset came, and sometimes they were in the
> streets before he could get back. (*I Am Legend*)

Or the beginnings of *Ubik* and *Solaris*, respectively:

> At three-thirty A.M. on the night of June 5, 1992,
> the top telepath in the Sol System fell off the map in
> the offices of Runciter Associates in New York City.
> That started vid-phones ringing. (Philip K. Dick)

> At 19.00 hours, ship's time, I made my way to the
> launching bay. The men around the shaft stood aside
> to let me pass, and I climbed down into the capsule.
> (Stanisław Lem)

For some authors of detective fiction, there almost seems
to be a rule about starting with the time and place of the
crime. But they might also choose a single element that conveys the force of the offense, as we see in this beginning by
Friedrich Dürrenmatt, which pretends to be conventional:

> On the morning of November third, 1948, Alphons
> Clenin, the policeman of the village of Twann, came
> upon a blue Mercedes parked by the side of the high-
> way right by the woods where the road from Lambo-
> ing comes out of the Twann River gorge. It was one
> of those foggy mornings of which there were many
> in that late fall, and Clenin had already walked past
> the car when he decided to have another look. He
> had casually glanced through the clouded windows
> and had the impression that he had seen the driver
> slumped over the wheel. Being a decent and level-
> headed fellow, he immediately assumed the man was

drunk and decided to give him a helping hand instead of a summons. He would wake him, drive him to Twann, and sober him up with some soup and black coffee at the Bear Inn. For while drunk driving was forbidden by the law, drunk sleeping in a stationary car by the side of the road was not forbidden. Clenin opened the door and laid a fatherly hand on the stranger's shoulder. At that moment he noticed that the man was dead. He had been shot through the temples. (*The Judge and His Hangman*)

There are few crime novels whose beginnings are free of clichés. Among the exceptions to this rule is Bernardo Atxaga, who shows us extraordinary characters and events as if they were the most natural things in the world:

The man known to everyone as Carlos realized that the icy sea he was contemplating was merely an image in a slowly fading dream, and he realized too—as one of the voices in his conscience kept reminding him— that he ought to get up from the sofa where he was lying, that he ought to go down to the hotel lounge as soon as possible in order to watch the football match between Poland and Belgium being played at nine o'clock that night, 28th June 1982. However, the area in his brain still oblivious to the dictates of his conscience felt the pull of the sea he was watching in his dream, and that free zone told him to keep his eyes shut, not to move, not to allow himself to wake up completely, but to enjoy the pleasant sensation of falling that was taking hold of him and turning him into a rock doomed to smash through the layer of ice and disappear beneath the waters. (*The Lone Man*)

And then, of course, there's Patricia Highsmith:

Vic didn't dance, but not for the reasons that most men who don't dance give to themselves. He didn't dance simply because his wife liked to dance. His rationalization of his attitude was a flimsy one and didn't fool him for a minute, though it crossed his mind every time he saw Melinda dancing: she was insufferably silly when she danced. She made dancing embarrassing. (*Deep Water*)

The beginning of *The Big Sleep* is as boring as can be, but the last line saves it. Philip Marlowe, the detective in seven novels by Raymond Chandler, describes the glorious weather (by now the reader is already bored), then goes on to mention that he's clean-shaven and well-dressed; after going into detail about even the fabric his socks are made of, he tells us why he's feeling so optimistic: "I was calling on four million dollars."

Some novelists, like Fernando Vallejo and Horacio Castellanos Moya, write that first phrase to grab the reader by the collar and not let go until the whole story is told:

Glad you could come, Moya, I had my doubts that you would come, so many people in this city don't

like this place, so many people don't like this place
at all, Moya, which is why I wasn't sure you'd come,
said Vega. (Castellanos Moya, *Revulsion*)

Less dramatically, history and geography have also been
used to create textual doors cut to size for each project:

Two mountain chains traverse the republic roughly
from north to south, forming between them a number
of valleys and plateaus. Overlooking one of these
valleys, which is dominated by two volcanoes, lies,
six thousand feet above sea level, the town of Quauh-
nahuac. (Malcolm Lowry, *Under the Volcano*)

Or:

There was a depression over the Atlantic. It was trav-
elling eastwards, toward an area of high pressure
over Russia, and still showed no tendency to move
northwards around it. The isotherms and isotheres
were fulfilling their functions. The atmospheric temperature was in proper relation to the average annual
temperature, the temperature of the coldest as well
as of the hottest month, and the a-periodic monthly
variation in temperature. The rising and setting of
the sun and of the moon, the phases of the moon,
Venus and Saturn's rings, and many other important
phenomena, were in accordance with the forecasts
in the astronomical yearbooks. The vapour in the air

was at its highest tension, and the moisture in the air was at its lowest. In short, to use an expression that describes the facts pretty satisfactorily, even though it is somewhat old-fashioned: it was a fine August day in the year 1913. (Robert Musil, *The Man Without Qualities*)

Or the way Truman Capote does it in his most famous novel:

The village of Holcomb stands on the high wheat plains of Western Kansas, a lonesome area that other Kansans call "out there." (*In Cold Blood*)

For stylists, the most important thing is that the novel's first lines announce its tone and form:

Stately, plump Buck Mulligan came from the stairhead, bearing a bowl of lather on which a mirror and a razor lay crossed. A yellow dressing gown, ungirdled, was sustained gently behind him by the mild morning air. He held the bowl aloft and intoned: —*Introibo ad altare Dei.* (James Joyce, *Ulysses*)

Showtime! *Señoras y señores.* Ladies and gentlemen. And a very good evening to you all, ladies and gentlemen. *Muy buenas noches, damas y caballeros.* Tropicana! The MOST fabulous night-club in the WORLD—*el cabaret más fabuloso del mundo*—where

performers of Continental fame will take you all to
the wonderful world of supernatural beauty of the
Tropics—*al mundo maravilloso y extraordinario y
hermoso*: The Tropic in the Tropicana! (Guillermo
Cabrera Infante, *Three Trapped Tigers*)

On the day they were going to kill him, Santiago
Nasar got up at five-thirty in the morning to wait for
the boat the bishop was coming on. He'd dreamed
he was going through a grove of timber trees where
a gentle drizzle was falling, and for an instant he
was happy in his dream, but when he awoke he felt
completely spattered with bird shit. "He was always
dreaming about trees," Plácida Linero, his mother,
told me twenty-seven years later, recalling the details
of that distressing Monday. (Gabriel García Márquez,
*Chronicle of a Death Foretold*)

The personality of the main narrator tends to appear in
these first lines. Like this example of naivete from Jorge
Ibargüengoitia's *Two Crimes*: "The story I'm about to tell
begins on a night the police violated the constitution." Here,
on the other hand, his narrator is an expert at leaving things
unsaid:

Where to begin? It's nobody's business where I
was born or who my parents were, or how many
years I went to school, or why I was appointed the
President's Private Secretary. However, I want to

make it perfectly clear that I was not born in a dirt-floor hut, as Fatty Artajo claims, and my mother was not a prostitute, as some have hinted; nor is it true that I never entered a schoolroom, but finished the sixth grade (with praise from my teachers, as a matter of fact). As to the post of Private Secretary to the President of the Republic, it was offered to me in recognition of my personal merits, which include impeccable etiquette that invariably arouses admiration and envy, unwavering honesty that has, on occasion, gotten me into trouble with the police, alert intelligence, and, above all, a pleasing personality that many envious people find insufferable. (Ibargüengoitia, *The Lightning of August*)

These strategies are always evolving. Nineteenth-century novelists circled like birds around their subjects, affording themselves the luxury of describing an entire town, a parade, or a wharf before getting down to business. There's the beginning of *The Red and the Black*, which waits an entire chapter before introducing the protagonist:

The little town of Verrières can pass for one of the prettiest in Franche Comté. (Stendhal)

A gesture Stendhal revisits in *The Charterhouse of Parma*:

On the eighteenth of May, 1796, General Bonaparte made his entry into Milan at the head of that young army which had shortly before crossed the Bridge of Lodi and taught the world that after all these centuries Caesar and Alexander had a successor.

And to which Dumas and Flaubert were no strangers:

On the 24th of February, 1815, the look-out at Notre-Dame de la Garde signalled the three-master, the *Pharaon* from Smyrna, Trieste, and Naples. (Alexandre Dumas, *The Count of Monte Cristo*)

On the 15th of September, 1840, about six o'clock in the morning, the Ville de Montereau, just on the point of starting, was sending forth great whirlwinds of smoke, in front of the Quai St. Bernard. (Gustave Flaubert, *Sentimental Education*)

Taking a bird's-eye view of the twenty novels that comprise Émile Zola's *Les Rougon-Macquart*, written between 1870 and 1893, you will see that most begin with an indication of the time and place, and of the identity of the character that the reader should get to know, while around the same time Jules Verne could grab the reader's attention by opening with his characters' shouts, as he does in *The Green Ray*.

While nineteenth-century novelists circled around their subjects, writers in the second half of the twentieth century liked starting in the middle of the action, giving the impression—as Simon Leys points out in a wonderful essay in *Protée et autres essais* (Proteus and other essays)—that the reader is boarding a moving train. J. M. Coetzee's *Disgrace* and *The Snow of the Admiral* by Álvaro Mutis are good examples of this:

> For a man of his age, fifty-two, divorced, he has, to his mind, solved the problem of sex rather well.

> Reports had indicated that a good part of the river was navigable up to the foot of the cordillera. It isn't, of course. We're in a flat-keeled barge driven by a diesel motor that fights the current with asthmatic obstinacy.

If we examine the long opening of *The Man Without Qualities*, we see that the initial impact doesn't come from the first line, but rather at the end of that immense introductory paragraph. We should not lose sight of the fact that, once our work is cast into the avalanche of the bookstore, we only have a few lines, if we're lucky, to catch the reader's attention.

Sometimes the first sentence isn't particularly effective, but it flows with such grace that before we know it, we're on to the second, and then reaching the end. This is true of novels by Jean Echenoz and Sándor Márai:

> "I'm going," said Ferrer. "I'm leaving you. You can keep everything, but I'm gone." And as Suzanne's gaze drifted toward the floor, settling for no good reason on an electrical outlet, Felix Ferrer dropped his keys on the entryway table. Then he buttoned up

his overcoat and walked out, gently shutting the front door behind him. (Echenoz, *I'm Gone*)

In the morning, the old general spent a considerable time in the wine cellars with his winegrower inspecting two casks of wine that had begun to ferment. He had gone there at first light, and it was past eleven o'clock before he had finished drawing off the wine and returned home. Between the columns of the veranda, which exuded a musty smell from its damp flagstones, his gamekeeper was standing waiting for him, holding a letter. (Márai, *Embers*)

The most famous opening of all belongs to a novel that was never written. Making fun of realist novelists, whom he saw as frivolous and insipid, Paul Valéry commented to André Breton that he couldn't fathom how anyone could write a phrase like "The Marquise went out at five o'clock." Breton, who shared Valéry's compunctions, thought that the novel promoted conformism in its readers. Useless information and the affectation of realism, so hostile to any aesthetic, intellectual, or ethical aspirations, seemed to him like signs of mediocrity and self-satisfaction, which could therefore only produce insulting books, ridiculous plays, and above all novels that render us docile. What, Breton wondered, does the series of clichés that is descriptive prose, that plain and simple communication of information without any freedom of spirit, have to offer? Where did the character's freedom go? Temptation? Desire? In the *Surrealist Manifesto*, the movement's leader forgot to mention that some writers did manage to escape the curse of the Marquise. Some, like Denis Diderot, managed to rouse the reader with a jab of their spurs:

> How did they meet? By chance, like everyone else. What were their names? What's that got to do with you? Where were they coming from? From the nearest place. Where were they going to? Does anyone ever really know where they're going to? What were they saying? The master wasn't saying anything and Jacques was saying that his Captain used to say that everything which happens to us on this earth, both good and bad, is written up above. (*Jacques the Fatalist*)

Picking up where Breton and Valéry left off, some twentieth-century novelists have discovered the value of having their narrators speak directly to the reader in the opening lines, forcing them to participate in the story:

> You are about to begin reading Italo Calvino's new novel, *If on a Winter's Night a Traveler*. Relax. Concentrate. Dispel every other thought. Let the world around you fade.

One of the legacies of the novel, from Jonathan Swift on, is opening with the protagonist's family tree and abridged résumé, until that legacy turned into a convention and writers like J. D. Salinger tried to escape its weight:

> If you really want to hear about it, the first thing you'll probably want to know is where I was born, and what my lousy childhood was like, and how my parents were occupied and all before they had me, and all that David Copperfield kind of crap, but I don't feel like going into it, if you want to know the truth. In the first place, that stuff bores me, and in the second place, my parents would have two hemorrhages apiece if I told anything pretty personal about them. They're quite touchy about anything like that, especially my father. They're *nice* and all—I'm not saying that—but they're also touchy as hell. Besides, I'm not going to tell you my whole goddam autobiography or anything. I'll just tell you about this madman stuff that happened to me last Christmas just before I got pretty run-down and had to come out and take it easy. (*The Catcher in the Rye*)

Others start out with an apparent simplicity that sometimes masks ironic or malicious designs; if you read past the first line, it's almost impossible not to continue on to the end of the paragraph, which, as is so often the case with this kind of writer, dangles a hook no one could ignore:

> Princess Springtime lived in an island paradise off the coast of Panama, in a lovely Palace of white marble.

She was young, beautiful, and single. (César Aira, *La princesa Primavera*)

Today, on this island, a miracle happened: summer came ahead of time. (Adolfo Bioy Casares, *The Invention of Morel*)

Following in the footsteps of François Rabelais and Miguel de Cervantes, a well-known Italian author pretended that the book he'd written was a document he had agreed to salvage:

> On August 16, 1968, I was handed a book written by a certain Abbé Vallet, *Le Manuscrit de Dom Adson de Melk, traduit en français d'après l'édition de Dom J. Mabillon* (Aux Presses de l'Abbaye de la Source, Paris, 1842). (Umberto Eco, *The Name of the Rose*)

Finally, there are beginnings that initially seem impenetrable. Even the best writers have crafted an excessively ornate door at some point—maybe because they are more relaxed, or inebriated with the joy of having just written one of their best novels yet. It's what happens in *The Tramp Steamer's Last Port of Call* by Álvaro Mutis:

> There are many ways to tell this story, just as there are many ways to recount the most insignificant episode in any of our lives. I could begin with what, for me, was the end of the affair but for another participant might be only the beginning.

And in *Tomorrow in the Battle Think on Me* by Javier Marías:

> No one ever expects that they might someday find themselves with a dead woman in their arms, a woman whose face they will never see again, but whose name they will remember. No one ever expects anybody to die at the least opportune of moments, even though this happens all the time, nor does it ever occur to us that someone entirely unforeseen might die beside us.

The poet Ricardo Yáñez would describe this tendency as "filigree covering the real," a tangle of signs growing over the "tree of life" like vines. Sometimes, when narrators introduce themselves in an overly complicated way, readers realize they're under no obligation to follow them, and they leave.

In closing, it's also important to note that the beginning should be closely tied to the last paragraph. Louis Aragon observed a tension between beginnings and endings, the tightrope across which the story moves. "I enjoy when the novel develops like a rainbow, when that defines the nature of its first and last lines." I'm going to look at just one case, so I don't ruin too many surprises. Here are the beginning and the end of Juan Rulfo's *Pedro Páramo*:

> I came to Comala because I was told my father lived here, a man named Pedro Páramo. That's what my

mother told me. And I promised her I'd come see him
as soon as she died. I squeezed her hands as a sign I
would. After all, she was near death, and I was of a
mind to promise her anything.

He hit the ground with a hollow thud,
crumbling as if he were a pile of rocks.

In the beginning we have a man holding the hands of his
dying mother, promising to make a journey and telling
her lies to keep her alive; in the novel's last line, we see
a character collapse and die despite his best efforts: this
is the moment the writer understands that the time has
come to release his creation, his novel, and let it fall. As if
lies were the lifeblood of fiction. As if the origin of every
novel were a lie that takes on alarming proportions before
speaking its truth. The novel, among other things, is a
preparation for life that death peeks through; it shows us
to look with reverence at the mundane. This brings us to
other problems that have to do with writing a novel, but
the beginning—at least the beginning of this book—is
behind us.

# The Novel as Automobile

A hundred years already, God damn it, a hundred years already, the way time passes.
—Gabriel García Márquez, *The Autumn of the Patriarch*

Jack Kerouac produced the 320 pages of *On the Road* in three weeks, typing out fifteen pages per day on a thirty-six-yard-long roll of paper, while Marcel Proust wrote the more than 1.5 million words of *In Search of Lost Time* over the course of fourteen years—advancing at a comfortable pace of three hundred words per day, if we were to calculate an average. Dostoyevsky was forced to interrupt his work on *Crime and Punishment* to whip up the nearly two hundred pages of *The Gambler* in the harrowing interval of twenty-seven days, by dictation, at the risk of losing the royalties to his entire body of work for nine years. Hemingway wrote *The Old Man and the Sea* in eight weeks, and Tabucchi penned *Pereira Declares* in three months, though both seem to have been composed at leisure after a long period of percolation.

While it is commonly thought that an experienced writer needs two years on average to finish a publishable novel, several innovators of the form took much longer: the 265,000 words of *Ulysses* cost James Joyce fifteen years of hard work; *In Cold Blood*, six; *Madame Bovary*, five; the imposing *Anna Karenina*, four; *Don Quixote*, something like eighteen, from the moment the idea occurred to Cervantes.

Books for the ages are written at different speeds. Louis Aragon could write a dozen pages per day of any of his novels-in-progress, while André Breton advanced at a snail's pace, producing half a page at most of *Nadja* in the same amount of time. On one hand, there are the goldsmiths who aspire to a page, or even half that, per day; on the other hand, those novelists who aim for at least two, but preferably four. To say nothing of Charles Dickens, Leo Tolstoy, Haruki Murakami, or Stephen King.

One tends to think of fiction as indomitable, but Hemingway never left his desk before he'd written his five hundred words for the day, and Georges Simenon, who could finish a novel in just a month, wrote a whole one in twelve hours while sitting in the front window of a bookshop, on a bet. When Simenon died, it was thought he'd only published 192 novels, but his last will and testament revealed that the Belgian author had also written and published another 176 under twenty-seven different pseudonyms.

Among Mexican writers, Carlos Fuentes took between six months and nine years to finish a novel; Fernando del Paso needed ten years on average to write each of his four monumental tales, each around one thousand pages long; Daniel Sada required six uninterrupted years for the nine hundred lyrical pages of *Porque parece mentira la verdad nunca se sabe* (Because it seems like a lie, the truth is never known), and Élmer Mendoza swears that he finishes the first draft of any novel in just over three months, but then polishes it for as many years as it takes. No one cares whether the novel they're reading was written quickly or slowly, all that matters is that it grabs them and takes them somewhere more interesting than their everyday life.

In order for our stories to become literature, the novel implies certain paradoxes: it demands that we forget about time yet also manipulate it, that we translate years of work into a single textual moment, and that we imagine time as a tangible thing. This is what Andrei Tarkovsky must have been thinking about when he asserted that time is "the flame in which the salamander of the human soul lives." What Tarkovsky says about directors can also be applied to novelists:

> What is the director's most important task? To sculpt time. Just like a sculptor, the director takes a piece of marble and, with the desired form in mind, removes all the excess, just like a cineaste takes a piece of time from the enormous mass of events of which existence is made, then eliminates everything he doesn't need, maintaining only that which will appear as the elements of the cinematic image. This process of selection is common to all the arts.

In his *Libro de quizás y quién sabe* (Book of maybe and who knows), Eliseo Diego acknowledges that to write is to capture a living being in a medium that underscores its appearance:

> Black, precise, delicate, the ant was trapped there in the amber; and here it is, some twenty million years later, like the frozen shard of some incredibly remote time . . . An unlikely if not impossible twist of fate brought the creature to the amber, and the amber to its printed image, and the printed image to your eyes, so it would be you longing to hear that whisper slipping between the impassive pines, out in the stillness, out in the darkness of time.

The theorists who have studied the laws that time obeys in the universe of the novel include Umberto Eco ("The Myth of Superman"), Roland Barthes ("An Introduction to the Structural Analysis of Narrative"), Gérard Genette (*Figures III*), and Mikhail Bakhtin, as mentioned earlier.

Bakhtin proposed the concept of the chronotope to describe the various combinations of time and space that different kinds of novels imply; Eco insists that for certain fictional characters to fully exist, they need to live in a dreamlike instant where time does not pass; Barthes invites us to question what he calls the "chronological illusion" of narrative prose. While Bakhtin shows us how certain elements are repeated in fictional narratives, to the extent that we can speak of *families* of novels connected by what they discover or contain, Eco reveals the logical contradictions that sound outlandish but allow a character to take on a life of their own. After convincing us that, from a narrative perspective, the thing we call *time* does not exist, Barthes invites us to take a work of literature and dismantle it, piece by piece. Genette is the only one, though, who managed to design a speedometer for narrative prose. In his *Discours du récit* (*Narrative Discourse*), Genette proposes comparing two elements: the duration of each event and the strategies employed in recounting it.

According to Genette, a writer can turn time into malleable material in one of only four ways.

In the first, the prose behaves like a mirror and faithfully reflects the important events of its imagined universe as they occur. With this approach, we are trying to create the sensation that we are narrating actions as they happen in real time. This means that the story has to move at a speed that corresponds to the intensity of the events being described; avoid spending much time on descriptions; and pay attention only to gestures, memories, and premonitions that will have a concrete effect on the rest of the plot. *The Three Musketeers* is one example of this approach, as are detective novels. We can also see examples of this "mirror speed" in works by Mario Vargas Llosa and Santiago Roncagliolo:

> The bus had stopped. He looked at the time: four in the morning. He saw the fogged-over glass in the windows. He wiped his so he could look outside.

Lashed by the wind, the rain fell horizontally. It was hailing. He noticed that the person sitting beside him had disappeared, along with a good number of other people. (Roncagliolo, *Red April*)

The second way to approach time is to reduce the narration of events to a minimum, like in a telegram. Reading this kind of story will take less time than the events depicted: the events evoked in *Chronicle of a Death Foretold* or Mario Bellatin's *Beauty Salon* unfold over more time than it takes to read the texts that contain them. Alejandro Zambra is adept at creating this kind of narrative, able to contain a larger story:

Julio avoided serious relationships, hiding not from women so much as from seriousness, since he knew seriousness was as dangerous as women, or more so. Julio knew he was doomed to seriousness, and he attempted, stubbornly, to change his serious fate, to pass the time waiting stoically for that horrible and inevitable day when seriousness would arrive and settle into his life forever. (*Bonsai*)

The third is the scissors approach: deliberately cutting out certain actions, even ones that might be central to the plot, forcing the reader to imagine secrets or loose ends as they run into gaps in the narrative. The narrator of *The Murder of Roger Ackroyd* omits, out of prudishness, an event that is key to solving the mystery and defines the climax of the novel. The old man in Kazuo Ishiguro's *An Artist of the Floating World* consistently avoids mentioning the episodes in his family life that he finds shameful or reprehensible, but the elegance with which these omissions are made allows us to imagine the enormous pain behind these events without needing to witness them.

We could call Genette's fourth approach balloon description: those stories in which the narrator painstakingly registers every detail of every object, character, or event in their fictional universe. Thanks to the work of Philippe Hamon, including *Du descriptif* (On description), we can reflect on whether description has evolved over the course of the history of the novel, and how it has been used. Writers today tend to treat description as if it were a microprocessor: trying to make it occupy the least space possible. In the nineteenth-century novel, however, the balloon was the go-to option; where description proliferated, the narration of events lasted much longer than the events themselves—a sequence the size of a whale to relate the shape of a button, which to some might not seem stylistically important or relevant to the development of the plot.

One could criticize Genette for being a bit slow, himself, to explain the cases he describes, but his contribution is indisputably solid. A novel might jump from one point of view to another, or even mix them, or it could be told backward, as Alejo Carpentier does, but the speed at which any of these hypothetical narratives advances always ends up corresponding to one of these four models. Even the narrator's memories and premonitions travel at one of these four velocities, which rarely manifest in a pure state but instead mix together according to the needs of each story or narrator.

In Latin America, these models can take on a remarkable level of complexity. Rulfo, for example, is an aficionado of ellipsis, as witnessed by the blank spaces he often slips in. But there are even more radical ellipses in Rulfo, which surprise us in the middle of a sentence:

> But just as [Fulgor] was leaving, the figure of Pedro Páramo uì had appeared.
> —Come in, Fulgor.
> This was only the second time they had ever met. The first moment he was the only one who took notice since back then Pedrito was still a newborn. And now this time. You might even count this as their first meeting. And Fulgor imagined he was speaking as an equal.

Pedro Páramo's entire childhood, adolescence, and early adulthood pass by in the leap from one sentence to another. Another example—less dramatic, but wilier:

> —Are you not dead? —I asked.
> The woman smiled. The man stared at me sternly.
> —He's drunk —the man said.
> —He's just scared —said the woman.

There was a petroleum lamp. A bed made of otate reeds and an equipal chair where the woman's clothes were draped. She was completely naked, the way God sent her into the world. He was as well.

—We heard someone moaning and banging his head against the door. And there you were. What's happened to you?

We'd heard nothing about anyone butting their head on any door, or most of the other things the protagonist does in the preceding pages, for that matter. Everything seems to indicate that Rulfo wanted to obscure Juan Preciado's most significant actions as he walks through Comala, so the only ones to perceive them and comment on them are the other characters, all ghosts.

Among the writers who stand out for their capacity for synthesis, we need look no further than Augusto Monterroso, who surprised even Italo Calvino with his speed: "When he woke up, the dinosaur was still there." It bears mention that Monterroso has described this text as a novel rather than a short story.

If microfiction was all the rage at the end of the twentieth century, Twitter became its vehicle at the start of the twenty-first. Writers like Francisco Hinojosa, Alberto Chimal, and José Luis Zárate speed along, following Monterroso. And then there's Jorge Harmodio: "And on the third day, curiosity revived the cat."

But breakneck speed and the recalcitrance of Comala's narrators aren't the only advances in narrative velocity made in Latin American fiction. In Argentina, they seem to have found an entirely new way to use a car.

At first glance, you might say that Borges is one of those writers who move in fourth gear, synthesizing everything, including descriptions, into phrases like "No one saw him disembark in the unanimous night." But it should be said that—with his cosmic enumerations that seem arbitrary, perhaps even sloppy, to an inattentive reader—Borges has invented a fifth speed. Who else could reveal a character's soul through an account of his life in the form of a list of objects and moments? The Aleph as narrative strategy.

The novel is like a car. Whoever wants to drive it needs to know all the possibilities its motor can offer. An inattentive driver is unable to maintain the proper speed, even if they were the one who originally set the pace: they suddenly accelerate and pass by the most interesting parts of the story, or they slow down and spend pages on anecdotes or details of minimal importance to the plot. Sometimes they foreshadow something extraordinary but forget to make that stop along the way, or else they remember giant chunks of their own past that have nothing to do with what's happening on the page. Keeping these four different speeds in mind helps us see if we've taken a wrong turn, or if the vehicle we're in has stalled out.

In the novel, time is a fiction just as carefully constructed as the plot, the characters, and the setting. It is the bedrock of the novel's invented worlds, those worlds through which we can better observe our own.

# A Theory of Evolution

Writers working on their first novel sometimes end up with a beginning that's as long as the hood of a 1970s car, revving their engines the way certain nineteenth-century novels do. It may take a writer several chapters to introduce us to the main character: they describe the house where the protagonist grew up, how to get to there, the challenges a visitor might face, and so on. Likewise, the endings of these first novels can sometimes be as ostentatiously long as the back end of one of those same vintage cars, full of postscripts, unnecessary explanations, and conclusions:

If self-reflection serves us, we gradually realize just how risky it is to test the patience of today's reader page after page. We trim the beginning and end, and our novels are suddenly a bit more compact. Sometimes they even begin in the middle of the action, and it's not uncommon for a story to come to a stop before the fate of the protagonist is revealed, allowing the reader to imagine the denouement, as is the case with many novels from the middle of the twentieth century.

At the start of the twenty-first century, writers like César Aira, Mario Bellatin, Álvaro Enrigue, Héctor Manjarrez, and Alejandro Zambra go further: they try to write in miniature, stripping their novels down to the bare minimum, to the point that their story is pure motor . . .

. . . with two seats at most: one for the author, and one for the reader.

# A Timeline of the Novel, 8th century BCE to Now

*Iliad* by Homer

*Odyssey* by Homer

*The Golden Ass* by Apuleius

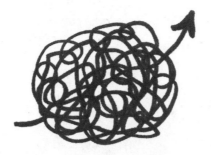

*Meditations* by Marcus Aurelius

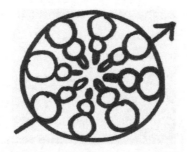

*One Thousand and One Nights*

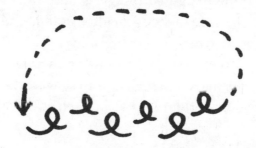

*Popol Vuh*

# Blind and
## So Mysteriously Reserved

In the real world, the objects around us seem impervious to our adventures and suffering, unmoved by our exploits; they also tend to keep pretty quiet. In the world of fiction, however, a desk can *intentionally* hide a secret, a murder of crows can mock a character, or an element of the landscape can comment on the plot or whisper the protagonist's true motivations in the reader's ear. In one of Murakami's novels, a plate of spaghetti announces the complicated series of events we are about to witness.

Though he imagined things as unsettling as a coin with just one face, a book made of sand, and a single point through which the entire universe could be seen, Jorge Luis Borges resisted endowing inanimate objects with consciousness. He preferred to suggest that, though they share our world, they live in a separate reality:

How many things,
Files, doorsills, atlases, wine glasses, nails,
Serve us like slaves who never say a word,
Blind and so mysteriously reserved.

They will endure beyond our vanishing;
And they will never know that we have gone.

This is strange, because rusted window grates, brick walls, stairs leading down to a basement, rose petals found in a book, or old-fashioned daggers never appear gratuitously in his short stories. Instead, they each fulfill a specific function: to amplify the traveler's melancholy, to set the mood for a fantastic discovery, or to help the protagonist express his thoughts.

In fiction, and especially in the world of the novel, objects have different levels of consciousness, as if they were animals at different evolutionary stages:

1. On the most elemental, mineral, Precambrian level, we have those base, inert objects that never do anything extraordinary but, when mentioned in sequence, offer a basic inventory that allows us to fill a void. Listing objects this way allows us to imagine a simple foundation, a backdrop against which the characters move. It is the first brushstroke the novelist offers to the reader's imagination, the stones that gradually construct the space. The objects in this first category will be depicted with varying degrees of detail, depending on the writer. As these descriptions grow, the objects become increasingly powerful and able to suggest something more.

2. Next, we have the nearly human level, at which objects take on a life of their own and react to the characters. Sometimes these objects become so important that the

landscape becomes a protagonist. In novels set in the jungle, elements of the landscape attack, mislead, and claw at the characters who dare to profane that space, sometimes even driving them mad, whereas they nourish, nurture, and help those who treat them with respect, as happens in *The Vortex* by José Eustasio Rivera, or even Luis Sepúlveda's *The Old Man Who Read Love Stories*. But this phenomenon is not limited to novels about the jungle. In Juan Villoro's novel *El disparo de argón* (The argon beam), for example, which is set in a small Mexico City neighborhood, when the protagonist needs to make a transition to a new phase in his life, the things that make up the landscape (bicycles, cars, bridges) sympathetically take up his cause and offer him an escape route. In Ibargüengoitia's fiction, on the other hand, it almost seems as if objects enjoy coming between the protagonist and the realization of his base desires.

3. There is a third level, which we might call poetic, in which certain objects, endowed with a unique sensitivity, understand and reveal a character's secrets. In general, what the novel is doing in these cases is translating the character's intentions into the physical form of one of the objects that lurks around or accompanies them. Sometimes these objects allow us to understand the character's essence:

- The Gamal sisters dream of getting married, but their surliness scares away their potential suitors: a screen of cactus stretches out in front of them.

- Juan Preciado believes he is going to inherit a fortune, but he discovers that his father thinks less of him than of the poorest mule driver: the crows mock him with their "caw, caw, caw."
- Georgina wants to flee a country in ruins but doesn't dare tell her suitor. Instead, she invites him to look at the billows of smoke rising from the Tamarere volcano—billows of smoke that do manage to escape.
- Doctor Pereira's health is so bad that even his fan is "asthmatic."

4. Sometimes certain concrete elements of the story offer a rich and evocative image of how the novel we are reading works, or how it was conceived: this is the metaliterary level of the narrative, when the prose through which the story is told opens its eyes and looks at itself. Objects can offer us a reflection, a commentary on how the plot was constructed. I think this becomes especially clear when we consider the vehicles that appear in certain novels.

At the beginning of *Strangers on a Train*, Patricia Highsmith pulls us onto a moving train as unrelenting as the events that are about to unfold. Will Bruno kill Haines's wife so he can marry his mistress? Will Haines return the sinister favor and agree to kill Bruno's father? The train careens forward as quickly as the whiskey-fueled minds of these two men who are both fed up with their lives. Something very similar happens in another detective novel, *Murder on the Orient Express* by Agatha Christie: the train keeps pace with Hercule Poirot's musings, as if its movement and the detective's deductive process were running on the same tracks. Each time he reaches an impasse in his thinking, the train stops, held up by snow on the tracks. And then there's the boat in *Love in the Time of Cholera*, which travels back along the same river like someone beginning to make up for lost time, and Álvaro Mutis's memorable tramp steamer, which gets held up just as the protagonist questions whether to go on with the story. It seems as if beyond these ships there is nothing at all, a void that the novel in our hands is fighting against.

5. Finally we have those greater objects: buildings. Through their descriptions of the architectural spaces where the story takes place, certain novelists manage to give us a sense of exploring, as we read, a more or less geometric space—a building with definite features that correspond to the impression the novels leave on their readers. The feeling of having inhabited that building or architectural space can be so clear that when they finish a particularly well-written novel, readers can draw its form: the home they lived in while they were reading.

Some writers set a rule for themselves when it comes to buildings: to have all the action of the novel take place within those immense objects, keeping the reader focused on what happens inside their four walls. We read a novel like Kawabata's *House of the Sleeping Beauties* and realize that the action has unfolded entirely indoors without our ever needing a glimpse of the outside world, and we feel we've just spent time in a form as perfect as a sonnet.

In the case of *Beloved* by Toni Morrison ("124 was spiteful. Full of a baby's venom.") the house itself becomes part of the action, as we will see.

6. Some writers need only mention a few unsettling objects to make us feel like we've picked up and traveled to a different dimension, a world that's neither true nor false, where we remain suspended until we learn how the story ends. In Álvaro Uribe's *La lotería de San Jorge* (St. George's lottery), for example, there is a tragic dimension, a sense of impending doom that carries over from one chapter to the next; it touches and determines the fate of the characters and draws to itself each of the objects that appear in the story, like the printed message at the beginning and the end of the novel. We live inside this uneasiness, this anxiety, until we hear that final phrase. It is these metaphysical objects that send the reader directly to the center of the story.

It should be said that these different levels of consciousness assigned to things can and often do coexist in the same novel. They crowd together harmoniously like the segments of an orange. No matter how different they are, they're never isolated: there are always communicating vessels, subterranean rivers that run from one level to another.

Why dedicate an essay to objects? Because the best fiction confirms an idea once expressed by Isak Dinesen:

focusing on the visible will reveal the invisible. And because it never hurts to take a look at the sinister, delightful, erudite, contemplative—and, above all, poetic—possibilities that objects offer when they follow a secret subset of the rules of physics: those that govern the unsettling form that is a good novel.

# How to Draw a Novel

No one ever stops to wonder whether novels think, yet they observe us and draw conclusions. Ever elusive, they adopt different forms and techniques, making it hard to trace and define them. We have to accept from the start that they have not one form, but many; that they have many ways of telling their stories, and realism is only one of these.

According to Thomas Pavel, in his monumental *Lives of the Novel*, novels not only think, they have their own philosophical system, similar to idealism—if idealism, rather than presenting a thesis, antithesis, and synthesis in its argumentation, presented characters, settings, and plot; if instead of reasoning, it told us stories that were impossible to verify.

The novel is not only the ideal setting for certain ideas to come face to face, it is also one of the few spaces with an indisputable geometry. Following Pavel, we need a taxonomy of the novel's varied forms. Whoever sets out to make this taxonomy will discover that, despite their astonishing diversity, all novels have something in common: a deep interest in stirring our emotions. If a good short story astonishes us once, the novel draws us in with steady doses of surprise: surprise at the forms its story takes, and at its unique way of moving forward.

We should not forget what Blanchot wrote in *The Space of Literature* about that slippery *something* behind all writing: "A book, even a fragmentary one, has a center that attracts it. This center is not fixed, but instead moves according to the pressure of the book and circumstances of its composition. However, this center is fixed in that, if it is genuine, it moves while remaining the same and becoming always more central, more hidden, more uncertain and more imperious. He who writes the book writes it out of desire for this center and out of ignorance. The feeling of having touched it can very well be only the illusion of having reached it."

To demonstrate that it is possible to represent the form of a novel, here is a system that allows us to do just that, sometimes with just a few movements of the pen:

1. Read the novel of your choice with this question in mind: What is its form? What is its disguise; what figure does it embody when it addresses the reader?
2. Everyday speech communicates things clearly; the novel speaks in a different way. Instead of stating ideas, the novel embodies them in the form of characters or style; instead of argumentation (thesis, antithesis, synthesis), the novel has its characters square off against one another.
3. Whereas nonliterary texts unfold in a linear way, sentence by sentence, the novel creates different paths that exist simultaneously but aren't necessarily headed in the

same direction or moving at the same speed. The novel branches out or braids together, shuffles or leaps forward, runs or stops, goes back to the starting block or jumps ahead to the end of the story.

4. When we finish reading a novel, we sense that every phrase has contributed to creating a form that reveals itself fully only in that final moment. Sometimes we are so aware of this form that we feel an impulse to draw.

5. In order to draw a novel, we have to depict the appearances and disappearances of its principal narrator, the alternation between different points of view, the relation between the central narrative and secondary ones, and, above all, the strategy: how the author decided to arrange the material, delaying certain elements, foreshadowing, concealing certain information.

Take, for example, a boring novel in which nothing happens in the plot or the writing itself. If we were to draw a straight line from the left side of the page to the right, representing the protagonist's trajectory, we would have the image of a failed and tedious novel.

—————————

On the other hand, if one were to place different obstacles (as is often the case in adventure novels) in the path of the main character—as happens in the *Odyssey* or certain tales from *One Thousand and One Nights*—the novel will gain a rhythm and will be more interesting and enjoyable to read. It will take the shape of a rollercoaster:

One should make sure that the challenges or obstacles are varied, so each tests a different aspect of the character. Even if after each of his adventures he is still lost at sea, unable to return home, it is not the same thing for the tireless Odysseus to blind the Cyclops as it is for him to convince Circe or Nausicaa to let him go on his way. Similar tales test different aspects of his character: his ability to stir the feelings of the Phaeacian king, his creativity in escaping from the cave, his talent in conquering a beautiful woman. Every loop on the rollercoaster is different, and yet we could say they all have the same shape:

After each of these adventures, we are returned to the original situation: Odysseus is still at sea, trying to find his way home. If we examine each of these contretemps closely, we discover that, despite their differences, they inevitably form this image:

That is, a digression. This is the novel's most characteristic movement. It can be found in its ancestors: it's present in *One Thousand and One Nights*, in *Don Quixote*, in Faulkner's *The Wild Palms*, and in Kafka's *The Trial*. If the novel were an animal, it would move by digressions.

Now, all novels may include digressions, but not all digressions are alike in their length or approach. For example, rather than making full loops that close quickly, some open a series of parentheses:

What novels of this kind, like Milan Kundera's *Life Is Elsewhere*, do is pull the brake on the linear story and gradually bring to light increasingly deep-seated aspects of the character's life, like ripples forming on a lake.

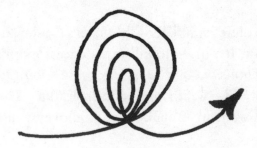

The moment arrives when we reach the center, and the parentheses begin to close. Perhaps, if we look closely, we might find that each parenthesis offers a poetic detail about the character or the plot: the sense we get of the character depends on the strength of these details. It goes without saying that every novel is a parenthesis, the outcome of a test, a period of transition in the lives of its characters.

The following could be the drawing of a *mise en abyme*, or any case where a secondary narrative is inserted into the main story, a novel within a novel:

In closing, I would like to offer a few examples. In its opening pages, *Pedro Páramo* seems to have the following shape:

But it doesn't take us long to realize that the protagonist dies early on, and that the dead tyrant whose name we invoke in the book's first lines (in the title, in fact) will take on more weight, more life, until he usurps the entire novel.

Now let's take a look at Gabriel García Márquez's *The Autumn of the Patriarch*:

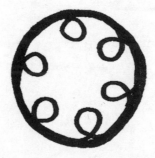

As you might recall, each chapter of that novel begins with an obsessive return to the same image—the vultures entering the presidential palace—and gradually the stories of the patriarch unfold, each of them nearly independent of the others, to bring us back in the end to that first image.

Regardless of how they moved through it, I've found that many readers of Cortázar's *Hopscotch* have drawn something like this when asked to take up this challenge:

On the other hand, Bolaño's *The Savage Detectives* appears to suggest this shape:

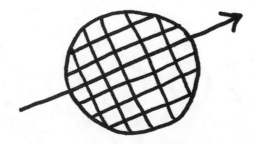

The diagonal line represents the poet García Madero's diary, interrupted by the dozens of characters that talk about Lima and Belano, though they may have met only once. At first glance, the central chapter in which the main action of this book occurs reminds us of a strobe light, like the ones you might find in a 1970s disco.

It bears mention that, as if the originality of this form weren't enough, Bolaño tended to write novels with shapes that varied widely from one to the next. To say nothing of the calculated madness of *Amulet, By Night in Chile,* and *Monsieur Pain*—madness with internal variations, as any reader can observe . . .

Bolaño begins *Nazi Literature in the Americas* as if it were a collection of independent stories, united by a shared theme:

Suddenly, though, in the last text (which is actually a short novel), he introduces us to the author of the stories, and a book that seemed like an encyclopedia is transformed into a novel—perhaps a practice run at *The Savage Detectives*.

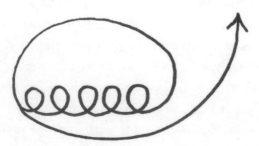

Another Bolañan shape that merits discussion is, of course, the form of 2666, in which the five parts that make up the novel can be read separately, though they share a setting, subject, and characters, and are interwoven to varying extents. "The Part About the Critics" and "The Part About Amalfitano" at the beginning of the book have little to do with the murders of women in Santa Teresa, which are more relevant to "The Part About Fate" and are the focus of "The Part About the Crimes." Finally, "The Part About Archimboldi" offers a full-length view of the mysterious author with whom the critics were obsessed, and returns to Santa Teresa to find the women's killer:

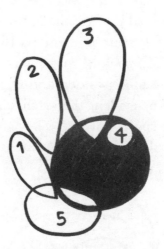

Several of César Aira's novels take a similar turn. They gradually move away from the main storyline until they form a single, powerful digression; when this digression deflates, instead of losing the reader's attention, it blows all that energy back at the main plot, strengthening it and giving it new momentum. Aira is a true master of digression, or, as he calls it, "the flight forward":

We should remember, now, that novels are not two-dimensional objects. If we were to take an X-ray of any of the books we just mentioned, we would see that they are not disinterested parties: the X-ray would reveal the lines of emotion that drive them. As Umberto Eco once said, the novel is a machine for generating agony.

If we were to film, in slow motion, the behavior of a novel, it would be evident that each has its own way of moving through space. Within its elephantine proportions, *Don Quixote* makes constant digressions, several of which are short novels unto themselves:

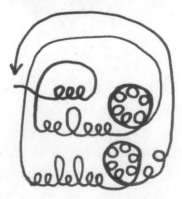

A novel told in counterpoint—like Mario Vargas Llosa's *Who Killed Palomino Molero?*, which is narrated by one character focused on the investigation at hand, and another who shares with him some of his most important memories—would move in this unusual but coherent way.

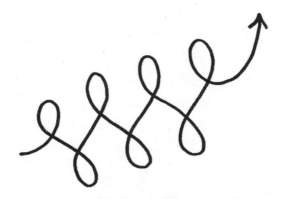

*The Feast of the Goat* would add another loop to the previous form, since it weaves in a third point of view.

If we're talking about complexity, two novels by Fernando del Paso have a lot to say. As the author himself has admitted, *José Trigo* has the shape of an ascent up a pyramid, followed, after a central chapter, by a descent:

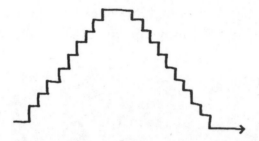

*News from the Empire*, for its part, offers us a monologue from the Empress Carlota, followed by three chapters that tend to work as perfect short stories. This unique figure is repeated as many times as the novel has chapters:

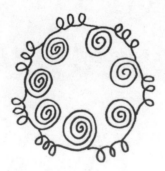

In my opinion, Horacio Castellanos Moya's *The She-Devil in the Mirror* has one of the most original structures of any crime novel. It consists of nine confessions made by a female character who is talking on her cell phone with her best friend. As the story progresses, however, we start to wonder whether the woman is suffering from some kind of hysteria, and whether the friend actually exists:

This story does not move like Ricardo Piglia's *Artificial Respiration*, another novel constructed from four long (and delirious) stories: the correspondence between Marcelo Maggi and Emilio Renzi about Enrique Ossorio; the delirium of Senator Luciano Ossorio; the delirious letters that seem to be sent from the future to a mysterious censor, Arocena; and the narrative of a Polish man, Tardewski, which includes stories from his companions at the café. Though everything seems to indicate that the novel will center on the story of the uncle, Marcelo Maggi, the story branches out and ends where it began: with a set of papers inherited under strange circumstances.

In one of his most famous essays, Jorge Luis Borges suggested that forms seek to enter the world through the artist's imagination. Some of these forms try discreetly and unremittingly to do so by crossing the threshold we call the novel, and some, very few, succeed.

# A Timeline of the Novel,
# 8th century BCE to Now

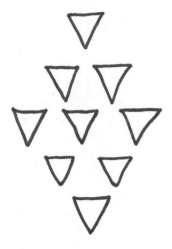

The short stories of Edgar Allan Poe

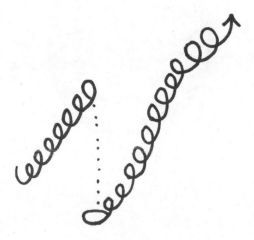

*The Count of Monte Cristo* by Alexandre Dumas

*The Metamorphosis* by Franz Kafka

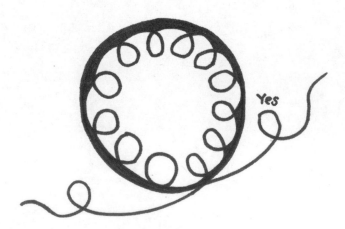

*Ulysses* by James Joyce

*The Great Gatsby* by F. Scott Fitzgerald

*Orlando* by Virginia Woolf

# Structure's Ghost

For Amy Hundley

Of all the ghosts that inhabit the novel, structure is one of the most elusive. It is also the most exquisite. It tends to appear in the work's earliest moments of gestation, when the author's intuition is vast, or right in the final stretch, when the final piece of the puzzle falls into place. It might take the form of a straight line, a chain of illusions, the branches of a tree, a circle that returns to its origin, an improvisation that rises like smoke and draws shapes in the air, a many-headed hydra, a chorus sung by many, a swarm of tempestuous memories, a river of surprises and word games, delicate berries from the forest or the daunting avalanche of fate, the struggle between heroes and villains, an equation rich in dramatic tension, or a mystery tackled by several minds.

And yet, none of these forms is possible if the fiction doesn't follow coherent architectural principles that add meaning to the story, stir our emotions, and avoid introducing random elements where none are called for. Contradictory as it might seem, there are specific places in the haunted house of fiction where the ghosts should appear. Every narrative should be designed so these seemingly spontaneous apparitions have the greatest impact as they go about their routines and show up at the precise moment the author conjures them. This is one of the greatest paradoxes that govern fiction.

One would have every right to believe that so much calculation and architecture are impossible and ill-suited to artistic creation, or even that analyzing the path taken by the narrative could be detrimental, but the interest in a story's structure is nearly as old as the first novels or Greek poems. What is Ovid describing in chapter six of *Metamorphoses* if not the essence of the art of storytelling when the competing Arachne and Minerva weave threads of their tales into their respective tapestries? And what, if not the earliest inklings of the elements present in the novel, does Longus describe for us in the prologue to *Daphnis and Chloe*?

One illustrious example of this can be seen in an eighteenth-century novel. At the beginning of *Tristram Shandy*, in the famous and brief fourteenth chapter of the first book, Laurence Sterne halts the narrative to sketch a bunch of scribbles as tangled as cords from a fallen spool; these are supposed to represent the path his story had taken up to that moment. Sterne describes a paradox that deserves to bear his name: each time he tried to make his narrative follow a specific path, the twists and turns of the story conspired to betray him, growing quickly in unexpected directions like rebellious vines, taking him further and further from his initial objective. This is why *Tristram Shandy* seems to be made from living matter, restless and insubordinate, that refuses to follow conventional paths or procedures.

Kurt Vonnegut did something similar at the end of the twentieth century in his famous discourse on the form of the novel, which appears in *A Man without a Country* as a text that begins, "Here is a lesson in creative writing." There, the author of *Slaughterhouse-Five* does not describe the direction of a story or the rebellion of the matter it consists of, the way Laurence Sterne does, as much as he depicts the changing fortunes of the protagonists of different works of fiction, and the rush we feel when we learn the details of their fate. Made with a single, fluid line, Vonnegut's diagrams offer three possibilities along the way: a fall, an ascent, and a narrative plateau without ups or downs. These three basic paths can be combined with one another; by charting them, Vonnegut managed to explain how most fictions work, from "Little Red Riding Hood" to *The Metamorphosis*. According to Vonnegut, in some stories everything is terrible at first and the protagonist seems to be in freefall, but then he finds a way to turn things around, his luck improves, and he gets what he was after: these are the novels with happy endings—if they're told well, they leave the reader happy. Then there are stories that start out well enough, but things go wrong: at first, we seem to be reading about a real winner, but then something happens, and the protagonist and his desires suffer an enormous reversal of fortune, falling far below his expectations with no hope of turning things around, despite his best attempts. These novels end badly, leaving a bitter taste in the reader's mouth, though sometimes with notes of perfection.

With his wonderful diagrams, Vonnegut shows that it is possible to draw the feelings provoked by the adventures and misadventures of a fictional character as if we were looking at them through a telescope. Sterne, on the other hand, holds a magnifying glass up to the digressions that the story's raw materials might insist on making. Broadly speaking, we get the sense, however, that the twists and turns of the stories we read can be represented with a single stroke. To illustrate this point, we're going to visit a few haunted houses, built between the nineteenth and the twenty-first centuries in the northern reaches of the American continent.

## The Legendary White Whale

Let's begin with a majestic novel that has no fewer than one hundred epigraphs, one of the most ambitious tales ever written, which demands weeks of attention from its readers, a story told in 135 chapters—41 of which don't actually advance the plot but instead interrupt it with essays about whale hunting. It may be hard to believe, but almost one-third of the narrative bulk of *Moby-Dick* is a direct assault on the most basic narrative principles, insofar as it brings the story to a grinding halt at some of its most exciting moments, as if an encyclopedia were taking over an adventure novel. The result is a novel just as monstrous and unpredictable as the monster being hunted in its pages.

As readers of Ishmael's diary know, this novel does not mention a single date but instead recounts the highlights of the adventure: how the sailors were interviewed and hired on Nantucket; under what conditions they shipped out; how many months they spent tracking whales; how they saw a giant squid; how many days on average it would take the crew of the *Pequod* to process and store each part of the whale; how they hunted their first sperm whale and how fiercely they fought over their prize with another ship that claimed it; how the *Pequod* crossed paths with the *Bachelor*, the *Rachel*, the *Delight*, the *Samuel Enderby*, and other ships that looked increasingly battered the closer they got to Moby Dick; how a harpooner named Queequeg killed a respectable number of sharks unassisted, and how another, named Tashtego, fell into the open cranium of a cetacean and was rescued from certain death by his shipmates; how young Pip went mad, left to his fate on the open ocean; why Ahab promised a gold doubloon to the first man to sight the white whale, and which crew member collected; how they were visited by an ominous waterspout, and how they listened for hours to the cries of shipwrecked sailors through a strange, impenetrable fog; how Fedallah prophesied Ahab's destiny and those three fateful days when three whale boats full of crew set out after the white whale and not one of them returned intact. Above all, the novel recounts how many days a man's soul can waver between good and evil before he faces his destiny.

*Moby-Dick* is made from two types of material. There are the chapters of unmatched velocity composed of pure action, where we follow the crew of the *Pequod* in their search for the white whale, living from one calamity to the next. And then there are the parts that halt the action of the novel to give us heavy doses of practical information. In the former, the story takes us to an unpredictable, violent place where each element of the landscape announces the evils in store for the *Pequod*: mysterious sailors emerge from secret cabins aboard the ship; false prophets foretell unparalleled horrors; a magus demands a nearly impossible ritual in order to defeat the white whale; and, in the novel's final pages, a desperate captain baptizes in the name of Satan the harpoon he plans to use on the leviathan. The encyclopedic chapters, on the other hand, tend to pop up unexpectedly and—after giving us a monumental knock with their tail—stop the story in its tracks and immerse us in an intensive course in whale hunting. Written in a wise and witty style, these chapters seem drawn from Melville's experience during his years on a whaling vessel and stand out for the elegance and erudition of their prose and, above all, for the narrator's enviably wry humor.

The problem, for many readers, is when these materials meet. How can we be expected to tolerate the interruption of a race between two whaling ships to catch the same sperm whale? Worse still, instead of this chase we're given an essay that lists the appearances of whales in paintings and literature throughout the centuries. Why interrupt a moment when the sailors are risking their lives to capture a monster of the deep to explain in detail how jurisprudence applies on the high seas, or to describe the industry-recommended way to carve up a whale? And, of course, who in their right mind would dedicate a whole chapter to the structure of a sperm whale skull while dozens of hungry sharks are fighting the whalers for possession of the beast?

In the first half of *Moby-Dick*, fiction and nonfiction compete for the reader's affections. The book's first chapters, which bubble over with excitement as our protagonist travels to New Bedford and from there to Nantucket to ship out with a whaling vessel, alternate with perfect little treatises on our image of the sperm whale: the imprecise paintings that try to capture their likeness and the legends that attribute magical qualities to their spouts, which few mortals have glimpsed. While Ishmael and Queequeg speed across distant seas, the narrator dives deeper and deeper into the smallest details so we know everything there is to know about this greatest of monsters when the time finally comes to face him. The line that traces this back-and-forth between speed and depth, between anecdote and information, would be a wild zigzag, like the kind a big fish cuts through the water on the high seas.

Disturbed by this strategy, many have given up on the book after a few pages, not realizing that its author is preparing us to hunt prey that uses two contradictory modes of escape: speeding away across the surface of the water, then suddenly diving into the deep. Little by little, the narrator turns us into the most uncommon of readers: fans of adventure who also embrace the adventure of depth.

Something strange happens right around the middle of the story: the sailors finally catch sight of the white whale—the monster they've been chasing from one rumor to the next, from one catastrophe to the next, for months on end. We've been warned of the approaching danger by mad prophets, magi, and the captains of other whaling ships that have lost boats full of crew to the white whale. But the novelist's technique suddenly changes the moment the whale is sighted, to the extent that time seems to stand still. If the first half of the novel gives us the history of man and whale over centuries, we are about to be given the story of these whalers in a flash. Though nothing signals that anything like this is about to happen, we suddenly leave Ishmael's head and his notes behind and are confronted with all the secret trepidations of the *Pequod*'s crew as, one by one, they explain to us what is going through their minds in that singular moment when they realize they are about to come face to face with their greatest fear. In this unusual chapter, eleven monologues of terror and awe, of curiosity and shock, pass before our eyes with the force of a crashing wave. The hermetic Captain Ahab, his first mate Starbuck, noble Stubb, beleaguered Flask, the harpooner Queequeg, the sailor Pip, the witness Ishmael, two anonymous cabin boys, and even the magus Fedallah all speak, one after another.

Things couldn't possibly go on as before after all these secrets are revealed, and the novel indeed undergoes a fundamental transformation: speed and depth board the same whale boat headed into the fray. Melville changes his strategy and displays his mastery of the art of digression. Once the white whale has been sighted, instead of inserting brief essays on whaling in the voice of an invisible narrator safely tucked away from the action, the author chooses one of the characters dearest to the reader (Tashtego, Queequeg, Stubbs, or Starbuck) and forces him into an extraordinary and dangerous circumstance in which his only hope of survival rests on his detailed knowledge of certain secrets of the maritime world. Far from interfering with plot development, the explanations that seemed alien to the central story and completely unrelated to the adventures of the *Pequod* become indispensable for understanding the complexity and charm of each particular challenge. The author is transformed, just like his readers. In the middle of his novel, Melville creates an addiction to the same notes that seemed like such a trial at first.

Whoever gets to the second half of the novel will understand how the narration of the *Pequod*'s adventures absolutely had to occur at the same time as the meticulous explanations of whaling in order to give us this story life-sized. In the second half of the novel, *Moby-Dick* is not made of oil and water, of story and digression: it is made from a single curious substance that is constantly bubbling over, advancing and exploding upward like whale spout. *Moby-Dick* looks like a novel, but it is actually a radical lesson in the beauty and necessity of digressions; it not only asserts the necessity of the digressions we call novels, it also asks us whether life itself might not be a novel of uneven and unpredictable proportions.

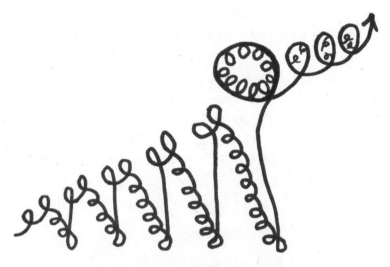

*Moby-Dick* by Herman Melville

## Novels of the Fall

After the whale-shaped novel, the downfall novel has captured the imagination of generations of writers in the United States. From Mark Twain to Toni Morrison, the most notable writers have shown how fascinating a person's ruin—and their attempts to overcome adversity—can be.

Downfall novels tend to begin with a setback for the protagonist: Tom Sawyer loses the affections of his beloved

Becky Thatcher and soon thereafter makes an enemy of
Injun Joe when he sees the man murder a former accom-
plice; Huck Finn, ostracized for being an orphan, helps
a slave escape and sparks the ire of his neighbors; Hank
Morgan, a disillusioned nineteenth-century man, wakes
up in the days of King Arthur and is forced to survive
in an even more inhospitable environment; Edward VI,
son of Henry VIII, dresses up as a young pauper who is
his exact double but discovers that by a twist of fate he
won't be able to end the game, recover his identity, and
return to the Tudor court. In *The Prince and the Pauper*,
the challenges our protagonists must overcome to get their
identities back are few, but they are massive, whereas in
*A Connecticut Yankee in King Arthur's Court*, our hero
is able to return to the nineteenth century but loses his
family in the process.

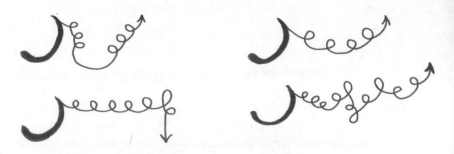

*The Prince and the Pauper* (top left), *The Adventures of Tom
Sawyer* (top right), *A Connecticut Yankee in King Arthur's
Court* (bottom left), and *Adventures of Huckleberry Finn*
(bottom right) by Mark Twain

Several characters in North American novels discover, in the course of their downward trajectory, an ability to defy the laws of the universe. Hoping to spend a glorious weekend in the bars and jazz clubs of Manhattan, the protagonist of *The Catcher in the Rye* runs away from the boarding school where his parents have left him, but his plans are ruined the moment he reaches the city: a prostitute and her pimp run a scam on him, a classmate rejects his friendship, the girls he wants to see aren't available, he can't hold his liquor, and he quickly loses most of his money. Consumed by the vertigo of his imminent entry into the adult world, Holden must sneak into his parents' home to borrow his little sister's savings. Just when things seem to be getting better, Holden finds himself on the verge of being discovered and has to flee. He knows it won't be long before his parents find out he's been expelled and send him to military school, which will increase the chances of his being sent off to die in combat like his brother did; in turn, he realizes two things: that he will inevitably turn eighteen and take that official step toward maturity, but also that he can stop telling his story whenever he chooses. And he does, just as his little sister is climbing onto a carousel. In this way, he is able to shake off everyone who was pursuing him, once and for all. With this unexpected literary device, *The Catcher in the Rye* reminds us that we are the stories we tell and that one of the greatest powers of storytelling is the ability to stop time.

*The Catcher in the Rye* isn't the only novel that manages to overcome its protagonist's downfall at the last moment, using fiction's greatest sleights of hand; this kind of trick can also be seen in *The Old Man and the Sea, A Confederacy of Dunces, The Sheltering Sky, The Dying Animal,* and *The Ordinary Seaman.* The protagonists of *The Great Gatsby, If I Forget Thee, Jerusalem [The Wild Palms],* and *In Cold Blood* are not so lucky.

In the case of Carson McCullers, the actions and reactions of the characters in *The Heart Is a Lonely Hunter* and *Reflections in a Golden Eye* are registered with such precision that it seems like their downfall is being witnessed by a sniper who is waiting for the exact moment to pull the trigger, but never does. She could stop time or interrupt her story but, just like J. M. Coetzee, McCullers prefers to depict her characters falling until they disappear into the abyss.

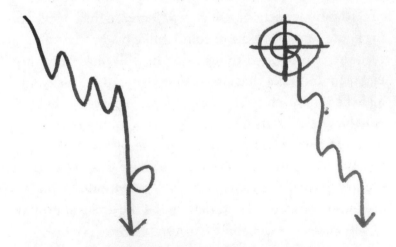

*Disgrace* by J. M. Coetzee (left) and *The Heart Is a Lonely Hunter* by Carson McCullers (right)

J. M. Coetzee's novels (*Disgrace* and *Waiting for
the Barbarians*) and Michel Houellebecq's
(*Whatever, The Elementary Particles*, and *Submission*)

For their part, the protagonists of Paul Auster's novels
offer a fascinating panorama of the different forms that
downfall can take: there's Jim Nashe, a gambler who has
been enslaved by an enigmatic tycoon and forced to construct a useless wall; there's a suspected bomber named
Benjamin Sachs; there's Marco Stanley Fogg, an orphan
determined to find his father and explore the world. Auster's
most memorable novels tell different versions, all of them
spellbinding, of struggle to survive. In their constant tug-
of-war between audacity and common sense, Paul Auster's
characters recall the adventures of *Don Quixote*, so much

so that his spirit seems to be distributed among many of them. In this sense, Auster wrote his own version of the book-burning episode in *Moon Palace*, of tilting at windmills in *The Book of Illusions*, and of general misgivings regarding human endeavors in *The Music of Chance*, *Leviathan*, and *The Brooklyn Follies*, among others. If we look closely at the shapes sketched by his novels, we see Auster's exploration of many of the great possibilities offered by the theme of downfall, and the tenacity with which his characters try to overcome the challenges that fate sends their way.

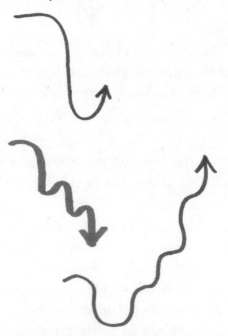

(From top to bottom) *Moon Palace*,
*The Brooklyn Follies*, and *Leviathan* by Paul Auster

This fierce struggle against adversity, this desire to lift one's eyes toward greener pastures when it seems all is lost, is characteristic of novels written in the United States. But there is something universal about it, too, which would explain the success this kind of story has seen over time.

## The Razor-Sharp Edges of Crime Fiction

From Mark Twain's day to the present, crime fiction has remained one of the most popular kinds of adventure novel. Crime fiction takes one of three forms, generally speaking, though each of these has been adopted by countless writers.

First: the perfect stories of Edgar Allan Poe, in which the presentation of the enigma, its investigation, and the solution are always fascinating thanks not only to the eccentricity of the investigator and bon vivant Auguste Dupin, but also to the strange minutiae of each case. This kind of story—with its polished prose, the growing intensity of its plot, and its surprise ending—leaves the reader with the same sense of perfection that a circle or an equilateral triangle does.

Second: the realistic, disillusioned crime novel. When it comes to hard-boiled fiction, talking about Dashiell Hammett is like describing primary colors. We could say that Hammett's novels, of immense literary quality, coined tropes that many later imitated: stories of

Quixotic detectives fed up with a culture of impunity and determined to mete out justice in a corrupt city; fights between two groups of gangsters provoked by an outside agent; dreams chased by police officers and criminals alike, dreams that ultimately prove as hard to catch as a cloud. In his novels—narrated by detectives, secret agents, or tough guys employed by gangsters—Hammett tends to apply extreme realism, which draws on his experience as an investigator for the Pinkerton Agency, to elaborate plotlines, rarely offering us a glimpse into what the protagonist thinks about the characters around him or what the outcome of his investigation will be. Hammett's protagonists are often hit men that the narrator prefers to keep at arm's length, not so much to hide their secrets as to step aside and let them speed along their way. Hammett's protagonists are impatient; as Sam Spade asserts in *The Maltese Falcon*: "We're sitting on dynamite and we've only got five minutes." His characters use their deductive skills, but they also use their fists, and—last but not least—they demonstrate a profound understanding of both human nature and the local underworld.

Another characteristic of Hammett's prose is his enormous talent for cutting every scene that lacks dramatic charge or slows the action of the plot. Hammett banished preambles, circumlocutions, and epilogues, leaving in his stories only the explosion itself:

*The Maltese Falcon* by Dashiell Hammett

With his brutal ellipses, Hammett forces his reader to imagine the details of a conflict that erupted right before each scene and will undoubtably continue long after the story ends. While your run-of-the-mill author of crime fiction tries to create ephemeral riddles, Hammett creates unforgettable slices of life told in language with a razor-sharp edge that cuts through the superfluous. In each of his scenes it seems that the characters are running in late and leaving just before a bomb goes off. And even if his characters talk like they just stepped out of a tough neighborhood, that dialogue contains extraordinary literary inventions; in Hammett's novels, the most sordid realism captures the pursuit of imagined beings and other chimeras. Magnificent illusions like the Maltese falcon and the thin man are made of the same material as that blind and monstrous creature we call Justice.

That the machinery of dirty realism should be activated in the pursuit of ethereal inventions is a stroke of genius rarely seen, even in the great tradition of North American detective fiction. No one carried this tradition on better than Raymond Chandler, with an even more Quixotic view of human justice, greater cynicism toward the lies of his detective's clients, and—one of the most influential traits of this genre—the flawless sarcasm of his Detective Philip Marlowe. Chandler pens conflicts worthy of a Greek tragedy and shrouds them behind layers of rumors and lies. His protagonists need to sift through corrupt witnesses who deny all wrongdoing and shift blame to characters who no longer exist.

The third and final direction that crime fiction has taken is to study the depths of the criminal soul. Joining Hammett's and Chandler's Quixotic detectives who make their way with sarcasm and quick fists are Patricia Highsmith's protagonists: killers and other criminals in danger, forced to escape arrest with masterful trickery. In *Strangers on a Train* and the extraordinary *Deep Water*, Highsmith descends all the way into the abyss of the thoughts and fears of her creations. While the narrators of your average crime novels immerse themselves just enough into the intrigue to catch their prey, never getting too far from the shore, Highsmith dives as deep as a whale into a sea of lies, bringing the reader with her to encounter unexpected landscapes and stories.

Highsmith wrote some of her best novels from the perspective of a con man: the astonishing Tom Ripley, a character used to committing the most disturbing frauds, but who also affords himself the luxury of helping out an old friend who's fallen on hard times. With Ripley, Highsmith deepened her exploration of what it means to live in a world of hypocrisy and convention. No one narrates the sea of lies more powerfully than Patricia Highsmith.

As we've seen in the previous examples, the greatest stylists of crime fiction craft their novels like urgent, rushed confessions. This quality is, without a doubt, one of the highest aims to which any novelist can aspire.

But there is a fourth option for the form that crime fiction can take: the literary thriller that gives us not only the detective's point of view but also a chorus of witnesses, that has a plot featuring extraordinary elements that defy common sense, and that uses every narrative resource to heighten the reader's sense of excitement.

One of the most popular types of literary thriller is shaped like an open pair of scissors: we are presented with at least four characters and their respective environments, habits, and problems. Some fall on the side of the heroes and the victims, others on the side of the wrongdoers and their accomplices. As they become involved in the central plot—in which the discovery of a secret, object, or person turns out to be pivotal—these characters gradually meet the protagonists of the surrounding storylines, who have the same intentions that they do, creating a first set of rivalries. Two or more characters might join together to fight against a common enemy, or they might compete against one another, and one of them might defeat or eliminate the others. Those who remain standing gradually come to understand that they should band together to overcome their rivals, and from that moment on they fight shoulder to shoulder to achieve this goal, until only one character or group is left, like at the end of a soccer tournament.

In other cases, the thriller is a journey through an onion, where the truth is hidden beneath countless layers of lies—Jason Bourne comes to mind. The task of the hero and their aides is to cross these layers one after another to reach the center of the story and, once there, avoid the great danger facing them so they can emerge unscathed to share the fruits of their investigations.

I am sure it would be possible to discover the strategies and evolution of this kind of thriller by observing the speed with which the different characters confront or eliminate one another in suspense novels written in the past few decades. This is the shape of novels like *Jaws*, *Jurassic Park*, *The Da Vinci Code*, *The Day of the Jackal*, and *Doctor Sleep*. But the endurance of this ambitious structure—which can, in a sense, be traced back to the *Iliad*—tells us something about our need for adventure stories and the constant battle between opposing groups.

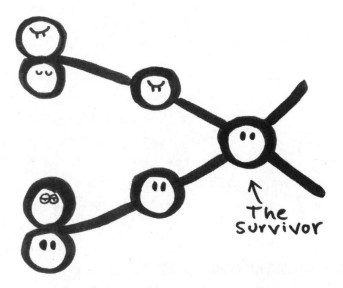

Thriller in the shape of open scissors

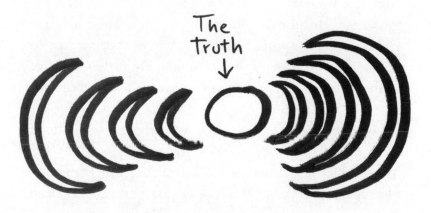

Thriller conceived as an onion

## The Poetic Novel and
## the Novel Made of Short Stories

In extraordinarily lyrical prose, *Fahrenheit 451* transmits in just a few lines the unpredictable way beauty bursts into the world. As the gruff fireman named Montag watches young Clarisse walk across a carpet of dry leaves shifting in the wind, Ray Bradbury's novel turns to the wonder of first times, in the form of childhood memories, the treasured moments of an adventure, or the pleasure of being alive. In prose of blazing intensity, Bradbury tells us a story whose climax is the moment the protagonist learns to read literature.

The twenty-seven stories that comprise *The Martian Chronicles*, for their part, form a unique archipelago: twelve short poetic texts interspersed among fifteen perfect and unsparing short stories. The poetic texts seem to comprise the diary of an immortal being who witnessed the arrival of humans on Mars and then, later, his own exile; the stories, meanwhile, appear to recount not so much the official story of the landing but rather a few of its most singular moments as they were lived by a diverse group of inhabitants.

In *Fahrenheit 451* we watch what appears to be a long short story turn into a novel before our eyes, while in *The Martian Chronicles* we witness how a collection of marvelous short stories, each of which could stand perfectly well on its own, stops being a bunch of islands and becomes a continent, thanks to the diary woven throughout. It might not be the biggest, but it is one of the most startling possibilities offered by the geography of Mars, in the hands of a skilled writer.

*Fahrenheit 451* by Ray Bradbury

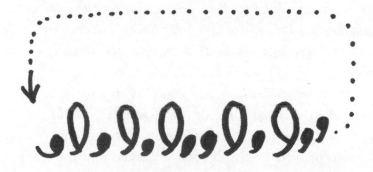

*The Martian Chronicles* by Ray Bradbury

## Zigging and Zagging

While most novelists focus on decorating gardens, Cormac McCarthy creates deserts. Instead of adding things, he excises words from his novels (*God, Benevolence, Justice*) and sees what the world would be like without them.

His stories can be summarized in a few lines, but they aren't easy to describe: two cowboys cross the border to get their horses back, which they do, but not without losing their souls; a hunter tracks down a she-wolf after miles of pursuit and is stalked by misfortune from that moment on; a hunter finds a treasure and is in turn hunted by a killer. Unlike Melville, McCarthy never makes his characters chase a white whale; they're all after small prey that represent, to these poor hunters, the chance to improve their lives or find meaning in them.

One of the greatest virtues McCarthy demonstrates in his novels is his ability to transmit his characters' sense of adventure. His heroes are observant and have excellent memories; they never lose sight of where the newcomer just holstered his pistol and don't hesitate to capture every word spoken by the countless storytellers who cross their paths.

In *Blood Meridian* and *No Country for Old Men*, McCarthy created some of the most terrifying figures in contemporary literature, while in *All the Pretty Horses* he also proved he could offer characters on the level of Tom Sawyer and Huck Finn, including a thirteen-year-old gunslinger who's afraid of thunder and a handful of cowboys who frequently risk their lives—here I tip my hat to Lacey Rawlins, Billy Parham, and the great John Grady Cole.

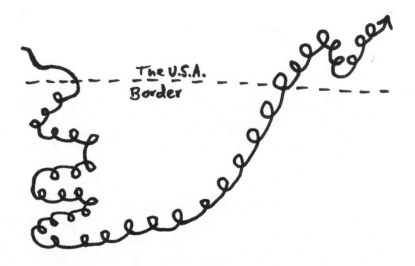

*All the Pretty Horses* by Cormac McCarthy

Convinced that a hero should cross borders, McCarthy exiles his protagonists from the relative security in which they've been living and forces them to travel, driven by a matter of life and death. At some point, after crossing over toward the furthest reaches of the south—never heading west or to a big city—his heroes tend to get lost or to lose sight of their objective. With few exceptions, those who manage to return to where they started from have to get past a customs agent—sometimes a Mexican hitman, sometimes the merciless Judge Holden. McCarthy's invisible customs checkpoints end up stripping his characters of what they most value in their lives.

In the arduous wanderings we see in his stories, those zigzags that move between disasters and dreams, his characters think they're exploring the desert, when it's actually the other way around. The reader is left to wonder how much cruelty, how much adversity the protagonist can endure as he follows his erratic path.

For his ability to hide the keywords behind his stories and to take us across borders and through mirages in a zigzag composed of tragedy and poetry, McCarthy is the greatest example of the wanderer's novelist.

## The Shape of Ambiguity

This brings us to the principle of uncertainty. Thomas Pynchon's novels usually revolve around a delirious individual determined to solve a mystery, who takes the reader along as he investigates a series of outrageous episodes involving the likes of Inamorati Anonymous or Heroin Users Liberation Kollective, the existence of V. or Trystero, and the location of the mysterious "black device" set into a V2 missile during World War II. Whether his novels center on a paranoid divorcée or a pot-smoking detective, Pynchon's characters find themselves dragged into gray areas steeped in ambiguity, and even his protagonists seem to be searching for the main storyline, which is usually hidden somewhere in a delightful but amoeba-like opening sequence.

They may seem to get lost along the way, but these stories only pretend to wander from the main storyline. It's their strategy. Convinced that to declare a truth is to lose hold of it and, likewise, that truth is too valuable to leave within reach of those who might taint it, these novels abandon the direct route in order to arrive at their unique style. Pynchon pretends to write harebrained novels, he even feigns giving up on the mystery, but in fact he is borrowing from the world's most accomplished roaming novelists and exploring the vast possibilities that this amoeba-like form affords him. His narrative strategy can be disconcerting at first, but as the reader begins to understand the rules of this Pynchonian architecture it becomes clear that there is a method to the madness of these constant digressions.

If we look at any of Pynchon's novels up close, we will see that each chapter consists of different stories, all of them absurd, which all offer a glimpse into our attempts to confront daily life. In the illustration below, we see how Pynchon avoids the central storyline, how he manages this through the exploration of miniscule subplots, and how this procedure gives us *The Crying of Lot 49*, for example:

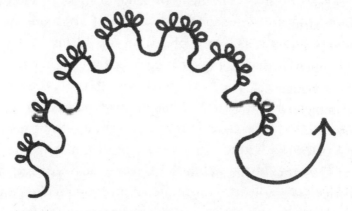

*The Crying of Lot 49* by Thomas Pynchon

Insofar as he presents us with what looks like a hare-brained account in order to pose disconcerting questions about a mystery, Pynchon takes huge risks with the reader and comes out on top. Employing the strategy of the false amoeba, he manages to portray that relative and elusive man-made invention we tend to call "truth." In his novels, Pynchon shows us that the only way to understand that illusion sought after by so many generations is by drawing the outline of the gaping hole that its absence leaves in its most imprudent, passionate, and even delirious pursuers.

## Novels Shaped Like Fruit

Adept at making their readers laugh and suffer, at surprising and shocking them, the most successful novels force us to drop everything and devour them in small portions, furtively, if necessary, over hours or days we pass with a sense of urgency, as if we were running out of time to unravel a mystery. The taste of some of these specimens is sometimes so intense that we can only consume them in limited doses, as is true of certain small fruits. No one could read them in a single sitting, even though they're not particularly long. The heart needs time to process what it reads—or what it sees, because in this type of novel, the characters appear right before our eyes, a feat of magic that comes with grace and literary precision. Any one of its chapters, chosen at random, would leave us feeling satisfied: each one provokes such a profound feeling that the reader has no choice but to close the book and come back to it later. To finish it in just a few hours would be to waste the opportunity to savor that uncommon taste for another day. We don't read these books; we seek them out the way someone might go out in search of their favorite food.

France had a novelist adept at creating these kinds of fruits, novels so moving and beautiful that you can't read more than a chapter each day. Émile Ajar (or Romain Gary, his real name) wrote this type of novel at least twice: first, in *Promise at Dawn* and then in *The Life before Us*. Both are stories of singular loves: in the first case, between a young immigrant and his mother; in the second, between a Muslim orphan and an elderly Jewish former prostitute. Both are stunning and deeply moving in the way these characters care for one another. In these novels about joy and poverty, each chapter tells a full story, each has an addictive flavor, and each is surrounded by similar chapters. The taste these leave behind might be sweet or bitter, but it is always exquisite, like those berries that grow in European forests and are divided into little drupelets that sometimes, when the fruit is exceptionally good, show us just how many layers can exist within a single flavor—or between the covers of a single volume.

On the American continent, *Beloved* is one of the greatest examples of this kind of story. Toni Morrison's famous novel is like one of the incredible blackberries that its characters pick from the field as soon as they're able to escape the plantation. From the book's first pages, the reader follows these narrators through the wildest brambles to taste another chapter, another point of view, another story, another adventure that allows him to experience all the facets of this exceptional flavor. In both parts of the novel, each chapter moves between the past and the present, as if the narrator were a drop of juice sliding across an unstable surface; but it is in the second part that the narrators' voices become truly unique. The stunning, ambitious first chapter throws us inside a haunted house during one of the most dramatic moments of the story; from this moment on, the past and present, what happened and what is happening, the characters' desires and what fate will offer them, are told at the same time. As the love story between a woman and a ghost progresses, the characters of this novel show us that dying is easy—what's difficult is living in a country that oppresses its people.

With their fragmented but coherent structures, their way of organizing the events described in each chapter, *Jazz*, *Beloved*, *Promise at Dawn*, and *The Life before Us* challenge conventional storytelling. They are more subject to the freedom of the novel than to the tyranny of linear time. Reading them is like listening to a storyteller who has just returned from a journey and is neither in a rush nor particularly interested in going in order, but who does offer us dazzling and uncommon stories. One of these might be very bitter; another, devastating; yet another might be a love scene or a childhood memory that makes us smile or laugh out loud.

For the organization of its chapters, which are drawn to a central character as to a magnet, and for the variety of flavors to be found within, *Beloved* is like a motley

blackberry with two clearly defined parts. In the case of
Émile Ajar, *The Life before Us* is as juicy as a raspberry.
These authors are completely different from one another
in terms of narrative strategy, characters, and themes. But
they both show, each in its own way, that sometimes the
novel is like a dictionary, in that it can't be read all at
once—but it is an unusual kind of dictionary that contains only the imagined beings that have sprung from the
author's mind. The novel knows everything about them,
but instead of offering us hard facts, it gives us captivating
stories, unusual sounds, and dazzling images; rhythms,
forms, and structures. Of all the different and unexpected
flavors life presents to us, some deserve to be written down
and remembered in the form of a story.

## Inventory

Considering how often their plots are driven by a character's downfall, a reader might think that novels are all
written about the same thing, or that there's only one
way to write them. But novelists take it upon themselves
to show just how many shapes this art form can assume:
defeats of epic proportions, fruits with new and intense
flavors, novels taken over by encyclopedias, dictionar-
ies of imagined beings, an archipelago that becomes a
continent, zigzagging paths and carousels on which our
protagonist lets out a delightful, delirious scream meant
to break through the night. North American novels are
adept at creating new forms, discovering new voices that
help us understand the world we live in.

# A Journey around a Tale

In 2003, Federico Campbell published *La ficción de la memoria* (The fiction of memory), a collection of essays about the work of Juan Rulfo. With Campbell's study and a copy of *Cuadernos de Juan Rulfo* (Juan Rulfo's notebooks) in hand, a group of writers gathered to compare three texts: the earliest sketches of *Pedro Páramo* as they appear in *Cuadernos de Juan Rulfo*, the draft of the novel that Rulfo turned in to the Centro Mexicano de Escritores (Mexican Writers' Center), and the final published version. What follows is the result of that exercise.

Fifty years ago, during his second fellowship with the Centro Mexicano de Escritores, Juan Nepomuceno Carlos Pérez Rulfo Vizcaíno—better known by his pen name, Juan Rulfo—began writing in a composition notebook the first chapter of a novel he had been thinking about for years but hadn't known how to approach. Rulfo imagined a man at death's door whose life flashes before his eyes as he lies beside a dead woman who speaks with others beyond the grave. Over the course of its different versions, the novel-in-progress was titled *The Deserts of Earth*, *A Star Beside the Moon, Murmurs*, and, finally, *Pedro Páramo*. Rulfo considered setting the novel in several different towns in southern Jalisco, where he spent his childhood, but ended up inventing a place that doesn't exist and events that never happened. Over four intense months, he wrote a first draft of more than two hundred pages, then spent the rest of the year cutting and rewriting until he ended up with a novel of less than one hundred. In this new version, a man arrives at a hostile town where people disappear as he walks down the street; he hears howling, but there are no dogs; he hears voices but can't tell where they're coming from. In the first pages of this novel, the protagonist encounters the ghost of a mule driver, the voice of a man who died by suicide, two coquettish dead women, and a man and a woman covered in something like a skin made of mud that crumbles at his touch.

If Juan José Arreola is to be believed, the structure of this novel populated by ghosts was decided during a game of ping-pong. Rulfo and Arreola were neighbors, and one night, in the grip of a professional crisis, Rulfo went to see his dear friend in the hope that he might help him make sense of the seventy-nine fragments that comprise the novel. Arreola took it upon himself to spread this version of the story: "More than a realist," he asserted, "Rulfo is a writer of fantasy, a writer both enlightened and blind. That is, he has stumbled blindly into the greatest writing of the literature of our day because the true artist is blind, not knowing where he is headed, but arriving all the same . . . Those of us who are from the same place as his stories and his characters can see how it has all become magnificent, poetic, and monstrous." For years, Arreola's description fed the misunderstanding of Rulfo as unsophisticated and telluric, intuitive and not very inventive, overcome by the magic of his own creation. The rumor spread by Arreola is an attractive one, but it is also false. As we now know, *Pedro Páramo* was not written despite its author.

The year is 1954, and it is midnight. Juan Rulfo is leaning over his kitchen table, writing a novel that still has not found its form. He will be there all night with his hundred pages, and at around five past six in the morning, Juan Rulfo will know he has finished his book. He thinks to himself that he'll finally be able to turn it in to the Centro Mexicano de Escritores, receive the final installment of his grant, and see the book published. He is satisfied. He's finished, so he doesn't care much what people might say about it; this is for the best, since in the years that follow some critics will see *Pedro Páramo* as a failure, as just another novel of the Mexican Revolution, as messy *costumbrismo*, and it is only thanks to a handful of astute readers that it will come to be seen as a great novel, a true wonder of verbal alchemy. Mariana Frenk, the novel's German translator, insists that *Pedro Páramo* should be counted among the great modern novels, alongside the work of Kafka, Faulkner, Proust, and Joyce. Rulfo's collected works might not add up to more than three or four hundred pages, García Márquez has said, but these are as vast and timeless "as what we have from Sophocles."

Comala, the world created by Rulfo, works like a living organism composed of artfully designed elements. The dead speak clearly to one another, but whisper to the living, who feel, rather than hear, these voices, like the ones that come to us in dreams. When the protagonist is literally dying from fear, one of his sinister hosts tries to initiate him in the customs of the world beyond the grave. In an impeccable Jaliscan accent, she tells him not to worry, it's just the way things are there: "This town is full of echoes. It's as if they were trapped in the gaps of the walls or beneath the cobblestones. As you walk, you feel someone following in your footsteps." This is why Octavio Paz wrote that his vision of this world is, in fact, the vision of another. According to Paz, Rulfo "is the only Mexican novelist who has given us an image—not a description—of our landscape," an image in which the author's personal intuitions and obsessions "are manifested in the rocks, the dust, the pirú."

It is quarter past six and the sun is coming up. Juan Rulfo stands and decides to go to the corner to buy some bread. Before he heads downstairs, though, we need to debunk three common myths.

First: More than one reader of *Pedro Páramo* has drawn the conclusion that the characters in the novel are Indigenous. But Comala's residents are of Spanish descent. Indigenous characters appear in just one short chapter in the novel, when they come down off the mountain to sell herbs under the arches of the town's gate. Rulfo always tried to correct this misreading, stating that there were no major Indigenous characters in the novel and that he'd never written any, at least not from their point of view, because he could never say how they think.

Second: The characters in the novel pertain to fantastic, rather than realist, literature. To quote Augusto Monterroso, "Years ago, people mistakenly saw Rulfo as a realist, when in fact he is a writer of fantasy." He goes on to say that Rulfo's ghosts

> differ from North American or European ones in that, in their humility, they do not try to frighten us, but simply want us to pray for them or help them find eternal rest. It goes without saying that these ghosts are poor, like the landscape through which they move; they are very Catholic and, above all, they are resigned in advance to our not giving them even the little they ask for. In short, the thing about Rulfo's ghosts is that they really are ghosts.

Third: Contrary to popular opinion, any attentive reader will see that Juan Rulfo is not a solemn writer. His work surprises us with evidence scattered here and there of a vast, cruel, dry sense of humor for which nothing is off limits. In his novel, Rulfo revels in delivering the ultimate, almost cosmic, punch line of a character who lost everything and still hasn't realized that he's dead. Rulfo's humor seems designed by his most downtrodden characters, who seem to us to already be dead, to welcome a new arrival to the circle they inhabit, to the land of misfortune. Rulfo's humor "allows him to explore the human condition at a distance, to balance the tension in the story, to save himself from pathos. It is a high form of empathy . . . in moments of grief or cruelty."

Now that we're alone, while Rulfo is at the corner bakery, I am going to venture an observation: I don't think anyone has pointed this out before, but in the surprise it generates, at our protagonist's unexpected revelation, the structure of *Pedro Páramo* recalls that of a North American novel published nearly twenty years later by another visionary author. I am talking about Philip K. Dick's *Ubik*, in which we learn early on that the astronaut who travels to the moon discovers with horror, upon returning to Earth, that the ground he walks on is not the same as it had been just a few hours earlier; he can't understand what is happening around him, and even the objects at hand lose their substance and vanish. Philip K. Dick's astronaut, like the man who travels to the Media Luna, enters a shifting reality in which nothing is as it appears. Philip K. Dick and Juan Rulfo tell the story of two fallen astronauts, each in his own lunar landscape.

In *Pedro Páramo*, the protagonist follows the arc of a stone cast into the abyss. At a certain point, the pebble that is Juan Preciado disappears from sight and, just as the character vanishes in the middle of the novel, his disappearance gradually causes the avalanche in which the novel ends. "He sets out to search for his father, and ends up killing his father," writes Emir Rodríguez Monegal; what was as mysterious as a dream becomes as clear as a demonstration. It doesn't matter that it is the mule driver

Abundio, and not Juan Preciado, who kills the despot; these characters are actually two sides of the same coin.

Rulfo's novel works like a set of Russian nesting dolls, one layer inside another, with the truth always hidden a little further in. As readers explore the cemetery that is Comala, they are surprised at every turn.

The novel begins with a mirage: Comala in its heyday, seen through the eyes of Juan Preciado's mother. She instructs her son: "There, just beyond Los Colimotes pass, you'll find a beautiful view of a green plain, with a bit of yellow from the ripening corn. From that spot you'll see Comala, turning the land white, lighting it up at night." Reality will disprove this noble image. As soon as he enters Comala, Juan Preciado discovers that the paradise his mother promised him is an empty town. And the first resident he encounters, a humble mule driver, shatters his hopes when he confesses that he, too, is Pedro Páramo's son.

Juan Preciado almost immediately sees a woman disappear before his eyes "as if she'd never existed." He hears voices that seem to come from nowhere.

The next person he meets turns out to be dead, as are all the other residents he runs into, but none of them want to acknowledge it. One after another they pass the buck—the deceased is always someone else, someone who isn't there, "as if being dead were a cause for shame."

Halfway through the book, something truly unusual happens: we are shocked to learn that Juan Preciado has been dead since the novel began, and that everything we've heard up to that point was a dialogue between his corpse and that of Dorotea la Cuarraca; they share a tomb, but we don't know who buried them. At this point, we have no choice but to keep reading until the end. With tremendous intelligence, Rulfo brought us to an unexpected dimension to tell us that the dead hate heavy rains, that they rattle the lids of their coffins, that their names don't matter to them, and that they like to recall stories from their lifetimes, as also happens in the best works by writers like Akutagawa, Bierce, Homer, and Dante. All this is both contained and concealed in the novel's first, magnificent sentence.

*Pedro Páramo* by Juan Rulfo.
A depiction of Pedro and his ghost.

### Pedro Páramo Was Born in Tuxcacuesco

Thanks to Federico Campbell and the literary critic Father Juan Manuel Galaviz, we now know that Pedro Páramo was born in a small town in southern Jalisco but grew up in San Gabriel and Mexico City. What I mean is: Rulfo would have been about six years old when his father was murdered, and he would soon lose all the rest of his closest relatives, one by one. As he revealed to Fernando Benítez and Elena Poniatowska, "My maternal grandfather died when I was four . . . My father died when I was six, and my mother when I was eight . . . In the meantime, they killed two of my father's brothers, and then my paternal grandfather died . . . Another uncle drowned in a shipwreck, and so from 1922 to 1930, all I knew was death." He goes on: "When my parents died, all I did was draw zeros in my school notebook, nothing but little marbles . . . I know we are all alone, but I really was, more than anyone." His classmates in San Gabriel remember little Juanito: "How could we forget that shy, teary little güero . . . he barely spent any time with the rest of the gang." His brother Severiano says that Rulfo enjoyed chatting with the farmers who worked on the property in San Gabriel. Then he would sit alone in the garden, spending hours lost in thought. He loved to read more than anything, he was a solitary, taciturn compulsive reader with no one to lean on. His distant relatives barely gave him the time of day and, instead of taking him in, sent him first to the Luis Silva orphanage in Guadalajara, where he had no friends and no one visited him, and then to the Seminario del Señor San Jose, also in Guadalajara, where Rulfo was immersed in the purgative and illuminative stages of spiritual life before making his escape. With no small effort, he learned the basics of accounting and found a job as a government archivist in Mexico City. There he "crashed" at the home of a surly and distant uncle, Colonel David Pérez Rulfo, who had fought the Christeros under General Ávila Camacho. He was a member of the Presidential Guard, but his proximity to the president did not help much when it came to finding his nephew employment; Rulfo ended up working in fields far removed from literature, even selling tires, before securing a position at the National Institute of Indigenous Peoples.

Conversation was never his favorite sport. After he became famous, he didn't love giving interviews, either. When Elena Poniatowska asked him, rather insistently, what he missed about the 1950s, Rulfo responded that the best thing about life back then was that there weren't any Polish reporters bothering him.

Rulfo left ten minutes ago and he hasn't come back yet. After the bakery, he must have gone to buy the paper, so let's make the most of his absence and have a look at his desk. On one side are drafts of his novel, the mistakes and the padding he would later cut; on the other, the final version. Now imagine that we're comparing these versions to see what he took out. I will limit myself here to discussing just three changes that seem particularly telling: one from the beginning, another from the plot as a whole, and one from the last paragraph.

Let's start at the beginning. In one draft, which was in fact published in the first issue of *Letras Patrias* in 1954, we find a completely different literary project. Instead of beginning with:

> I came to Comala because I was told my father lived here, a man named Pedro Páramo. That's what my mother told me. And I promised her I'd come see him as soon as she died.

The young Rulfo wrote:

> I went to Tuxcacuesco, because I had been told that my father, a man named Maurilio Gutiérrez, lived there.

Totally different from the version we know by heart. What's Tuxcacuesco? And who is Maurilio Gutiérrez? Instead of saying *I came*, this narrator declares that he *went*, and instead of being *here*, Comala is *there*. The history of Mexican literature would have been different if this narrator had not been *in* Comala. And the name Maurilio Gutiérrez seems like a parody of itself: no self-respecting murderer could have that name. Nonetheless, the fearsome tyrant Maurilio Gutiérrez did in fact exist, and he committed numerous atrocities. It seems that Rulfo based him on a certain José María Manzano from Ciudad Guzmán, a bloodthirsty man who was known to bribe officials and steal his neighbors' land; in short, a man who is not remembered kindly, a man who was said to have made a pact with the devil because gold doubloons would appear beneath his horse's hooves . . . Or perhaps Rulfo based him on his own grandfather, Carlos Vizcaíno, who was so wealthy at one point that he, too, was said to have made a deal with the devil.

As for the town of Tuxcacuesco, as Federico Campbell reminds us in his study, it is located in the state of Jalisco, not far from where Rulfo lived. It gets very hot there, but not as hot as in Comala. As the popular poem goes, "Zapotlán, Heaven on Earth; San Gabriel, almost Heaven; Tonaya is Purgatory and Tuxcacuesco is Hell itself." Rulfo must have considered each of the towns near San Gabriel to see which one might serve as the setting of his novel; towns which, starting from San Gabriel, Rulfo drew in a clockwise circle: Apulco, Tuxcacuesco, Sayula, Tapalpa, Jiquilpan, San Pedro Toxín, Tolimán, Chachahuatlán, La Agüita, La Piña, Tonaya, Totolinizpa, Autlán.

As if that weren't enough, the tyrant in this first version was in love with the beautiful and unattainable Susana Forster, perhaps inspired by Celia Mejía, a girl with blue eyes who played with Rulfo during his childhood in Apulco. Where was the young writer hoping to go with this novel that was set in Tuxcacuesco and mentioned a real despot? Was he about to invent the nonfiction novel at the same time as Truman Capote in the United States? Perhaps it was these detours that led the other fellows at the Centro Mexicano de Escritores, including Alí Chumacero, Ricardo Garibay, and Luisa Josefina Hernández, to see Rulfo's early manuscript as a pile of disconnected scenes, and to think that the young writer should pursue other career options. Anyone would have said the same.

Luckily, Tuxcacuesco, Maurilio Gutiérrez, and Susana Forster became Comala, Pedro Páramo, and Susana San Juan. If the novel originated with that fearsome landowner who lived in Tuxcacuesco, we should be grateful to Juan Rulfo's sagacity for guiding him away from writing a realist novel—or even a social realist novel—and toward a work of profound originality. But let's get back to the manuscript.

If we look at all the changes that were made from one version to the other, we notice that Rulfo shaped his novel like a sculpture. Octavio Paz believed that the true biography of any writer is their body of work. Through the words Rulfo added, excised, and transformed, we can learn who he was, or who he was when he wrote his novel.

Let's take a look at the middle of the draft. Judging from the edits, Rulfo was not insensitive to the comments of his peers. We know that he didn't want to repeat the mistake he made with *El hijo del desaliento* (The child of dejection), a novel he abandoned after reading it one day and finding it verbose, cerebral, and soulless. He saved only the chapter titled "A Piece of the Night," which we can read now as a story—according to him, a very bad one.

So: from one manuscript to the next, Rulfo eliminated redundant words that lengthened his sentences, detracting from their power and music. His edits were aimed at perfecting the sound of the lines and making the dialogue more concrete, so the action would directly affect the visible actors and the story would take on new life. He also removed all historical references that would allow a reader to situate the novel in a specific time. Most of the references to the Mexican Revolution, for example, only fit in when the project was still at its most nebulous. Then he eliminated references to real people and places to create an imaginary territory in which he could move freely, without any need to be faithful to Mexican geography. Under this system, entire towns in Jalisco disappeared, and he ended his flirtation with the reality of the world around him. This change is fundamental, and it is perhaps the most important secret when it comes to manuscripts. The only one who didn't fare well was Don Maurilio Gutiérrez, the capo from Tuxcacuesco.

To be honest, I'm getting a little worried about Rulfo. He left home twenty minutes ago and still hasn't returned. Maybe there was a long line at the bakery, or maybe he stopped off for a quick game of ping-pong with Juan José Arreola. Or maybe the murderous Maurilio Gutiérrez, hungry for revenge, laid a trap to send him to the moon and Rulfo, like Juan Preciado, can't find his way back: he leans against a tree and the tree doesn't exist; he knocks on the door of a building and it's as if he's knocking on air. Instead of running, he moves in slow motion like an astronaut nearing the moon. He will quickly discover that he is, indeed, walking on an asteroid, and will feel like he can't breathe. Our only hope is that, in that precise moment, the little girl Celia Mejía will take him by the hand and lead him back to Earth. That she'll say to him:

"This way, follow me," and Rulfo will walk obediently behind her, never looking back.

Rulfo enjoyed going for walks. He would sometimes take his camera with him and take remarkable photos, but most times he would just go out alone, like most of his creations. Except Macario, a sedentary creature with a restless mind, Rulfo's characters are always on the move. Practically all of them are in motion, and it's because Rulfo's sense of fate means that his characters are always on the verge of tragedy: man is on the bottom, and the gods or those in power, those who cause pain, loom above. The best example of this is the father in "You Don't Hear the Dogs Barking," who carries his son—who is both injured and a murderer—to get him medical care. Trying to avoid passages in which nothing happens, Rulfo ended up right at the core of his characters. He used to say: "I jump straight to the moment when the action begins, when something happens to the character and he has to react, to look back on the events of his life." And yet, although his characters are nomadic, Rulfo does not tell us where they're going or where they come from. He presents them to us suddenly, "cast into a hostile world." As Manuel Durán writes, "Rulfo's characters—unaware, neglected, clumsy, overwhelmed—barely know who they are or what is happening to them . . . we feel we know them better than they know themselves, and we want to help them." But they don't listen to us. The characters in *Pedro Páramo* and *The Burning Plain* rarely ask themselves, "Who am I?" but if they do, the answers are usually unpleasant.

Rulfo once confessed: "I start by imagining my character, I simply imagine a character and try to see . . . where he will take me if he follows his path. I don't try to direct him, I follow." Once he imagined his creations, Rulfo would not try to build up their appearances; instead, he erased until he was left only with their perceptions. "Rulfo sets his characters loose on the pages of his books without any physical or spiritual description. What's more, they don't have a name for pages on end. In this way, what the character loses in terms of the body that characters in realist novels have, he unquestionably gains in an interiority oriented toward the mysterious." Instead of recounting the protagonist's background, of presenting him in the middle of his story, Rulfo introduces him already inside the tomb, after the story has ended. His characters are ageless. As García Márquez has said, "I always thought, a purely poetic intuition, that when Pedro Páramo finally managed to bring Susana San Juan to his vast kingdom on the Media Luna, she was already seventy-two years old. Pedro Páramo must have been about five years older than her. The drama actually seemed greater to me, more terrible and beautiful, if it was speeding toward the cliff of an unrelenting senile passion."

In just a few pages, Rulfo presents us with some fifty characters who appear only once, but who stay with us forever. The man who is hanged so his land can be stolen. The woman who runs a hostel after dying by suicide. The man who tells his wife, "Tonight I'm going after the calf," and never returns. A young rapist astride a galloping horse.

A girl trapped in a well . . . We have to imagine each of them, to do half the work that would originally have been done by the author.

Rulfo believed that the most important part of the novel was the imagined events, not the opinions of the author, which he avoided including. He disliked meddling narrators, or ones who turned novels into therapy sessions. Rulfo's narrators tell us only what is absolutely necessary "without the character ever analyzing his emotions, or the novelist doing it for him." The novel is not about writing everything that passes through our minds.

He told Joseph Sommers that he had never worked with direct autobiography, because the characters he knew in real life didn't offer the reality he needed, but his imagined characters did. He laughed at those who saw the novel as a transposition of events from real life, a story that was supposed to depict a real place and the people who lived there. To him, literature was fiction and, consequently, a lie. When the work is cohesive, it contains the author and their ideas about the art of fiction, so why repeat these and hobble the plot? "One should be wary of novels that try to teach us a lesson," he explained; "every book with a point of view communicates that, since every book is the entirety of a human life." As such, he cut out his personal ideas and opinions, all "lifeless" characters and long passages, grandiose language and gratuitous adjectives—all of which, according to him, ruined what was essential to the work. Margo Glantz has said that Rulfo rid his manuscript of explicative outgrowths, and that he mercilessly cut "any word or action that might annul the impact of death."

As you will almost certainly have noticed, Rulfo never uses affected language, and he avoids putting elevated words in the mouths of taciturn peasants. Instead of beating us over the head with one narrator, there is no principal point of view in *Pedro Páramo*: the center is everywhere. With great humility, each narrator steps aside so their figure won't block the action. Rulfo's similes are so precise that they go unnoticed. Let's take a look at one of these, which he corrected over and over. In the first pages of the novel, Juan Preciado makes a macabre statement when talking about his mother. When he arrives in Comala, he says: "I had imagined I'd see the place of my mother's memories, of her nostalgia, a nostalgia of tattered sighs. She was always sighing, mourning the loss of Comala, hoping to return. But she never came back. Now I've come in her place. And I come bearing the same eyes with which she saw these things, because she gave me her eyes to see." Rulfo states, outright, that the man is carrying around the eyeballs of his mother—eyes that can see. What I see in those eyes is a great surrealist detail, artfully concealed. Whoever doesn't believe me should reread the novel, paying special attention to those crows crossing the sky and mocking Juan Preciado with their "caw, caw, caw."

"What I didn't want was to talk like a book," Rulfo has said, "I didn't want to talk the way people write, I wanted to write the way people talk." The only time this novel employs literary language, as a matter of fact, is when the powerful despot recalls his childhood emotions.

## A Nocturnal Riddle

Ladies and gentlemen, this essay is about to end and Juan Rulfo still hasn't returned. Given that it's quarter to seven and we have no time to waste, we're going to jump to the final question: What are Rulfo's characters? Voices? Bodies? Souls?

For Fabienne Bradu, the residents of Comala are not so much voices as they are a kind of echo: whispers that no longer belong to the body from which they were separated. The dead identify one another by the stories they tell, not by their voices, which offer no clues. In this single novel, then, we have a cast of characters who each have a corpse, a voice, or an echo, and a wandering soul that resents the body. The effort invested in creating these characters can be explained by the fact that in *Pedro Páramo* reality always reaches us through them: we rarely witness the action itself, what we get is a memory of the action. Every landscape, every fact in Rulfo's novel is filtered through the consciousness of an imagined being.

A careful rereading of *Pedro Páramo* reveals each soul to have a different personality from that of the body it belongs to. In Rulfo's worldview, the soul could be separated from the body, and even resent it, like the internal gods described by the Greeks. Another of Rulfo's paradoxes can be found in the tomb shared by Juan Preciado and Dorotea, when he is frightened by the sound of footsteps above them ("It feels as if someone were walking on top of us"), and his companion, who is more experienced in these matters, advises him to relax and take it in stride ("It's time to stop being terrified. No one can scare you anymore. Try to think pleasant thoughts, seeing as we're going to be buried a long while here in the ground.") But why is she more experienced, if they buried her after Juan Preciado? Shouldn't she be the one who is afraid? Then again, of course, up to this point it is Juan Preciado and his initiation into death that we have been following.

In conclusion, as he edited, Rulfo put his manuscript to the test of irrefutable logic, of internal coherence in all its details. Nonetheless, the novel presents certain paradoxes and questions that the reader must resolve. For example: Who is Miguel Páramo's mother? Dorotea la Cuarraca, who misses her lost son? Why do so many of the dead argue amongst themselves over who will care for Juan Preciado? Are they vampires, fighting over their prey? And: aside from the episode in which Pedro Páramo is an apprentice in a telegraph office, where does he spend his adolescence and adulthood? Who were the shameless youths that so scandalized his father, Don Lucas Páramo?

For a long time, my biggest questions about the novel came from its beginning and end. Let's take a closer look at Abundio the mule driver, the character who brought us to Comala: Why didn't he say that he was the one who killed the despot? Abundio was already dead when he met Juan Preciado, and he had already killed Pedro Páramo. Why not confess it? Was he being cagey? Had he forgotten? Or was it that the murder hadn't happened yet? As the Jesuits know well, those who say no more than is absolutely necessary do not incriminate themselves. Perhaps, when interrogated by the protagonist, Abundio fell silent out of cynicism, acknowledging the cacique's death but not his own hand in it. It is also possible, though, that his silence was the result of ignorance: he didn't know about it because the murder hadn't happened yet. Did he need to pass some point of no return, some temporal border between the living and the dead, before he could reveal his truth to Juan Preciado? Rulfo is suggesting either that the dead can forget or that they try to manage their image through hypocrisy and lies. Perhaps, like good Zen masters, they understand how useless it is to explain death to the living, so they prefer to guide them toward their own encounters with that experience out of the goodness of their hearts. There is, however, another option, and it is the one I prefer. Perhaps—and I don't mind this idea at all—the character who met Juan Preciado isn't the real Abundio but rather his soul, tossed there dry and terse, dismissive of the history of the body it belonged to. In any case, we are dealing with an alternate universe, a reality that leads us to the very fair question: Is *Pedro Páramo* a mirage, a nightmare, or a hallucination? Let's not forget that the novel begins with the mirage of Comala and ends with Abundio the mule driver's hallucination: we are in the realm of ambiguity.

Another shadowy incident is the murder at the end of the novel. One of the characters, who has been drinking pure alcohol, stabs another without realizing it. Later, it seems as though nothing has happened, as though it has just been the old man's nightmare; this is when someone arrives and wakes the old man up. But the novel still has one last surprise in store for us. The first time I read the novel, its last page bothered me, and for years I believed that Rulfo had overdone it with the darkness. When I read the earlier version, I saw that Rulfo had written much more than what he published, but that he'd cut—with enviable perspicacity—everything that might illuminate the action too much. If it were a film, we might say he got rid of the reflectors. To commit a crime, you need the same shadows that Cortázar and Borges laid intentionally, deliberately, over the most unsettling areas of their stories. To describe a battle, the writer must reflect the battle; to transmit fear, the artist's language should be the language of night.

In the old version, the one with Tuxcacuesco and Maurilio Gutiérrez, Rulfo offered extensive explanations of the crime, enough to satisfy any writer of crime fiction. But when he was about to turn the manuscript in to the Centro Mexicano de Escritores, he must have thought better of it and decided that all those details about how the body fell and in what position would foreclose too many worlds, entire universes pulsing beneath the surface of that dark paragraph, so he took them out. By removing those explanations, by operating in calculated darkness,

Rulfo not only makes us feel Abundio the mule driver's confusion after drinking countless servings of alcohol, he also offers the reader multiple worlds, simultaneously. In that moment, the poor orphan who wanted to write about Tuxcacuesco created the Media Luna and, with it, a form of the modern novel: the novel that depends on the reader to decipher what the author conveys in a whisper. Maybe Juan José Arreola was right, after all, when he said that Rulfo was both enlightened and blind, that while he was searching with his head in the clouds, he stumbled upon the half moon.

Ladies and gentlemen: it's seven o'clock sharp and Juan Rulfo is about to return. In a few hours, once he finishes his lunch, he will turn in the draft of the novel. *Pedro Páramo* will be published a few months later, on March 27, 1955. When it first appeared, some called it a failed story about the Revolution; today it is read as one of the most important novels of the twentieth century.

This essay ends as Rulfo opens the door. You might think him a figment of our imagination, but it was he who invented us, the ones standing in his home, the readers of his novel.

# Novelesque Excitement

Toward the end of the nineteenth century, people were said to lead novelesque lives if they traveled extensively, experienced major twists of fate—at times disastrous (and someone would come to the rescue), at times lucky (in which case an enemy would try to destroy them). In any event, their lives were full of surprises, adventures, interesting anecdotes; protagonists who placed the most daring bets, laid it all on the line. The novelesque was at its prime: no one would have associated it with distraction, or called it boring, or outlandish.

Then, in the second decade of the twentieth century, as Thomas Pavel shows us in *La pensée du roman* (The thinking novel), came the great novels that sought to be more like poetry: Joyce, Proust, Kafka, Faulkner, to name just a few, followed shortly thereafter by a long train of imitators who, in their attempts to emulate their predecessors, managed to write some tremendously boring books. Adventure novels seemed to be the last bastion of surprise. As a result, people began to describe the novelesque as not having its feet on the ground.

A story is novelesque when it provokes in the reader, at regular intervals, the burning question: What will happen next? This question is as powerful as a wave: it lifts us high, pauses for a moment, takes our breath away, and unfurls onto the sand, or another wave, with a crash before disappearing. It's strange: when we talk about a novel, we remember the emotion it produced but never the nearly minuscule strategies that built up our interest throughout. Of an enthralling novel, we remember—at most—the emotion and the suspense, that private pleasure it generated in us, the moments when we suffered because of a character's impending doom; we don't remember the techniques used to produce those sensations.

According to Raphaël Baroni, one of the theorists who have studied the curiosity sparked by fictional narratives, the tension we feel when reading a story is also a poetic effect, the result of well-crafted intrigue. For Baroni, tension mounts when the reader has to wait to see how the plot will be resolved, and this waiting is marked by enough uncertainty that the denouement sparks an intense reaction.

Though a far cry from novels focused on developing a highly literary language, several early twenty-first-century television shows brought back the novelesque in the nineteenth-century sense—its constant surprises, its strategies for holding the reader's interest—and, in doing so, revealed to practitioners of the form just how much they had forgotten of this essential aspect of their art. And they did something else: returning to this essential element of the nineteenth-century novel, they turned the novel into a popular product that is also undeniable in its artistic refinement, able to captivate the most demanding novelist.

Can a writer learn from these series? Imitating, mathematically or systematically applying these novelesque approaches very rarely does any good. What does work is something else, and even the much-maligned crime novelist knows it. Patricia Highsmith once put it this way: "The novelist's secret resides in his individuality, in his personality. We're all different from one another, so it is up to the individual to express that which makes him different from everyone else. This is what I call the exhibition of oneself. But there is nothing magic to it. It is simply a form of freedom—a freedom with direction."

As the poet Ricardo Yáñez describes it: holding our most sensitive ear to our best voice. And following that voice, no matter what challenges we need to overcome along the way.

# A Method for Measuring Novelesque Excitement

1. Read any novel.

2. Mark the events that most grabbed you with the symbol of your choosing (it could be one or five stars, for example, according to their intensity): Will the hero betray his partner and friend? Will he cheat on his girlfriend or wife? Will he steal from his own mother? Will he be caught by the police, or will he manage to escape to a foreign land with his lover?

3. Now draw a graphic representing these moments. The line should ascend with each moment that stirs your emotions: you'll see that the more the novel grabs you, the more you worry about the fate of the protagonist, the meaning behind the adventure, in such a way that the drawing will keep moving upward—unless the story suddenly goes off course. This may be why the last pages of a good novel strike us as the most accomplished and irresistible, the ones we can't put down.

4. Now, examine your graphic and try to identify what kind of question the narrator in each of these peak moments

generated in you. (Will he find La Maga? Will Juan Preciado get his inheritance? Will he manage to escape from Comala? Will young Pedro marry Susana San Juan? Will he ever win her love? Will the Count of Monte Cristo get his revenge?) By identifying and examining the different kinds of questions a writer inspired in you, you will very likely be able to learn two significant things: how novelesque that writer is and what strategies they employ, on one hand, and on the other—if we like the book and repeat the experiment the following year—how deftly, distractedly, or deeply we read at any given moment.

# Device with Lions

For a while now, I've had a recurring dream about a device with lions. It's always basically the same, with slight variations. In the latest version, I find myself in a desert landscape, a savannah fit for survival of the fittest. The action begins as I see myself in a group of people running down a kind of hallway; along this hallway are twelve rooms, one for each month of the year. Each room contains a lion. We can see them because the doors are made of a material that is both transparent and solid enough to contain the beasts.

There are people with me, mostly strangers: faces you might see out in the street. We are a large group running in a line as if we were on our way to work. Every so often a door opens and a lion leaps out to devour someone. Everyone panics. Then a number is assigned to the one we lost and we gradually forget their name. The group keeps moving along the hallway, and by the end of the day we've gone all the way around.

Today, it happened to someone right in front of me. I hadn't noticed it before, but in here we're treated like a mindless, nameless flock destined to die. This is how the building is constructed, in its cruel perfection.

But the architecture doesn't explain everything. We suspect that magic is also involved, because after each lap we stop using one word. I never would have believed how quickly we would forget them, or how much poorer we are with their loss. Maybe this is why some of us have begun to sob.

No matter what our detractors might say, we haven't given up. We've tried everything in the different versions of the dream: from escaping the building to shutting the animals in. No one wants to die, but no one ever explained how to stop the lions, and the walls are very high.

Many succumb to desperation or indifference. None of this is our doing, and we don't deserve it. Though maybe it was the years we spent ignoring the existence of those lions that allowed them to impose themselves as they have.

This device is sturdy and long-lasting. Perhaps the worst is yet to come. On days like this, nothing produced by the mind or spirit seems like it could ease the pain. But then another night comes when we return home, disappointed and exhausted, and realize how much we need a mythology, how much we need novels that talk about those who were trapped here before us, and their lucky or naïve attempts to find their way out.

# A Timeline of the Novel, 8th century BCE to Now

*If I Forget Thee, Jerusalem* [*The Wild Palms*]
by William Faulkner

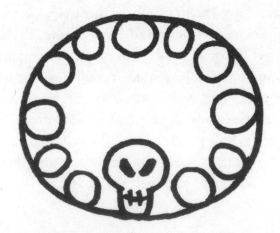

*Under the Volcano* by Malcolm Lowry

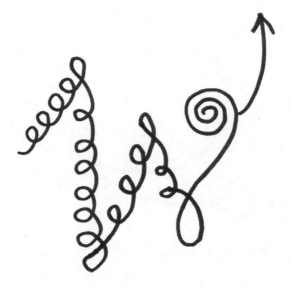

*The Catcher in the Rye* by J. D. Salinger

*The Old Man and the Sea* by Ernest Hemingway

*The Long Goodbye* by Raymond Chandler

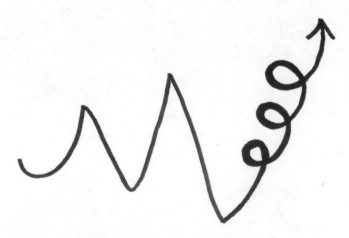

*To Kill a Mockingbird* by Harper Lee

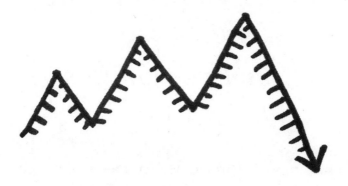

*In Cold Blood* by Truman Capote

# Insults and Images

In one camp, there are the detractors—usually poets, but also short story writers—who have hurled some pretty amusing insults at the novel. Valéry, Breton, Borges, and Maupassant have accused it, respectively, of usurping the sacred place of poetry, of neutralizing our capacity for revolt, of needing to include filler, and of being, therefore, boring by nature; it has also been accused of being formally impudent, of not having any rules. Many have called it the bastard child of literature and argued that it isn't worth the reader's attention; others have said that its genre is ambiguous, shapeless, amoebic, a far cry from the perfection of the sonnet. After pointing out its apparent frivolity, they have demanded that it take up the causes of its day, find new ways to tell a story and transform itself endlessly, or else stick to the demands of realism: describing a character or studying a passion.

In the other camp are the practitioners: stubborn creatures with little propensity for definitions or canonical rules, but with an undeniable capacity for work. Instead of defining the novel, they offer us a series of images—that sometimes coincide with the insults hurled by its detractors.

## Stendhal's Mirror

Notable among the images that novelists have created to explain the form is Stendhal's famous mirror. The French writer described the novel as "a mirror strolling along the side of the road. At one moment it reflects the azure skies, at another the mire of the puddles at your feet." There is something unsettling about this image, if you look at it closely: the mirror is walking on its own, without the assistance of any human hand. Stendhal is suggesting that the novelist is something like a monstrous creature, able to register everything with uncommon precision.

Not only can it move independently and reflect both the blue of the sky and the puddle by the side of the road, Stendhal's mirror aspires to capture everything, and is also obligated to show a different, enigmatic reality where things are the same as in our world, but also are not. As Sartre himself once wrote, "A novel is a mirror: everyone says so. But what is it to *read* a novel? To jump into the mirror."

Objectivity in recounting what happens in the mirror has always been a goal for those who narrate imagined lives. Just as Flaubert claimed to read passages of civil law every morning to steep himself in the concise and neutral style he needed to record his stories, Zola dreamed of writing sentences that were "like a house of glass" and that afforded him that much-desired neutrality. Some, beginning with Flaubert himself, have insisted that the author, in his work, must be like God in the universe, present everywhere and visible nowhere.

Everyone in the habit of making this type of mirror gets the same complaint: unlike sonnets, plays, or short stories, the novel lacks a single well-established form that would allow one to judge its degree of perfection. This complaint has been voiced by the common reader and specialists alike.

## A Monstrous Form

It's strange, but whenever someone describes a novel they didn't like, they say that they couldn't make heads or tails of it. Some even draw an imperfect body with those characteristics, which might have extra limbs or suffer from horrible asymmetries, a kind of poorly stitched Frankenstein's monster assembled from different cadavers, as if the novel were supposed to be made in the image of the human body. In its lack of harmony, however, this uneven anatomical figure reminds us that in a strict sense, "there is no such thing as a pure novelistic language, because there is no such thing as a pure novel. The novel is a monster, one of those monsters that man accepts, feeds, and keeps at his side; a mixture of heterogeneities, a domesticated gryphon," as Cortázar asserted in one of his last interviews.

In André Gide's *The Counterfeiters*, one character rejects the idea that the novel should always be faithful to reality, that this monster should be assembled from slices of life, as the naturalist school wanted: "The great defect of that school is that it always cuts its slice in the same direction: in time, lengthwise. Why not in breadth? Or in depth? As for me, I should like not to cut at all."

*Dracula* by Bram Stoker

*Frankenstein* by Mary Shelley

## Boring Material

Another common complaint regarding the novel has to do with its tendency to include boring information, typically concentrated in unnecessary descriptions. Borges was one of the first to launch this attack. These detractors, who were not always wrong, ignored the fact that many of their contemporaries wove their descriptions directly into the plot, making sure that they did not slow down the story. Flaubert disclosed to Sainte-Beauve as early as 1862 that "there is not one single isolated, gratuitous description in my book; each serves the characters and has a distant or immediate effect on the plot."

For the surrealists, descriptions were nothing but filler. One of the novelistic strategies that irritated them the most was the tendency of certain writers to stop the action each time an important character appeared demanding a portrait or a description. Fed up with this, Breton suggested that the novel should trade those boring descriptions for photographs.

Even before the novel was so viciously attacked by the surrealists, Mallarmé had tried to finish it off. When André Ibels asked him in 1898 what he thought of novels illustrated with photographs, he answered that he thought novels should not come with illustrations, that whatever the book evokes should come from within the reader. If a writer felt compelled to include photos in their novel, Mallarmé said, "Why not a bit of cinema? Its combination of text and images would replace the content of the book, to good effect."

No one questions the fact that characters in a novel pass through different stages and face challenges. A novel that presented only one emotion, a single note all the way through, would be incredibly boring. Maupassant insisted that a novelist should "start at a specific moment in the life of the characters and carry them, through natural transitions, to the next stage of their existence." In a letter to Louise Colet from June 25, 1853, Flaubert asserts the necessity of integrating the different phases of the novel, and of having them develop in harmony. In this letter, the author of *Madame Bovary* speaks of "phases," as if every novel must include different stages in sequence, like the phases of the moon.

## A House Made of Bricks

Detractors and defenders alike recognize that one of the novel's identifying features is its freedom in developing these phases: this is the source of its astonishing diversity. No matter how difficult it is to make the bricks from which the novel is constructed, or how artistic or experimental the use of these bricks might be, the novelist seeks to build "a formidable, amorphous mass," as E. M. Forster describes it in *Aspects of the Novel*.

It is natural to associate writing a novel with bricklaying. Henry James does so in his preface to *Portrait of a Lady*, to discuss the laborious process of extracting, carrying, and organizing each element of a novel. García Márquez himself has described writing novels as laying bricks, while writing short stories is more like pouring concrete.

In this famous preface, James elaborates further on his image of the novel as a house. He admits that, for him, the technique used for telling the story depends on the point of view selected:

The house of fiction has in short not one window, but a million—a number of possible windows not to be reckoned, rather; every one of which has been pierced, or is still pierceable, in its vast front, by the need of the individual vision and by the pressure of the individual will.

According to D. H. Lawrence, these houses should be constructed in a way that excites the reader. "The novel," he writes, "is the one bright book of life. Books are not life. They are only tremulations on the ether. But the novel as a tremulation can make the whole man alive tremble. Which is more than poetry, philosophy, science, or any other book-tremulation can do."

## A Laboratory of Truth

With its unique way of communicating to the reader, with the demands of its prose, the novel produces a singular kind of knowledge. Michel Butor sees the novel as nothing less than a "laboratory," because it allows us to explore the depths of a story and then share the results. Many agree with him, including Juan Ramón Ribeyro in *Prosas apátridas* (Stateless writings):

> To write is not to transmit knowledge, so much as it is to access knowledge. The act of writing allows us to grasp a reality that had previously appeared to us in a partial, veiled, fleeting, or chaotic way. We

discover or understand many things only when we write them. Because to write is to scrutinize ourselves and the world around us, using a much finer instrument than invisible thought: the visible, reversible, implacable, graphic thought of the alphabet.

## A Labyrinth

When someone is starting a novel or trying to find meaning in one already underway, it's not surprising that labyrinths come to mind.

In his treatise on the subject, *The Labyrinth in Culture and Society: Pathways to Wisdom*, Jacques Attali describes the labyrinth as a complex path, closed in by walls, that presents at least one entrance and the way to an exit or the center with no signs to indicate which direction to take. According to Attali, every narrative that depicts a labyrinth invariably recounts a journey in which the hero faces a test, uncovers a secret, and experiences some kind of resurrection. As such, in Attali's view, the labyrinth helps people find meaning in their own destiny, helps them hold on to the hope of achieving some ideal before they die.

The image of the labyrinth has also illuminated the writing of novels. The members of Oulipo, for example, describe the challenges that have interested them since the sixties as follows: "Oulipian literature is a literature of constraints, and Oulipian writers are rats who construct the labyrinths from which they will try to escape." These labyrinths, according to Raymond Queneau in his *Abrégé*

*de littérature potentielle* (Compendium of potential literature), are formed of "words, sounds, phrases, paragraphs,
chapters, books, libraries, prose, poetry."

Labyrinthine, too, seemed the answer provided by
Marguerite Duras when a young Enrique Vila-Matas
asked her what it took to write a novel. Duras, tired of
this kind of question from the strange fellow who rented a
room from her, scribbled out the following list on a piece
of paper and threw him into the street.

> 1. Structural problems. 2. Unity and harmony. 3. Plot
> and story. 4. Time. 5. Textual effects. 6. Verisimilitude.
> 7. Narrative technique. 8. Characters. 9. Dialogue.
> 10. Setting(s). 11. Style. 12. Experience. 13. Linguistic
> register.

As Vila-Matas attests in *Never Any End to Paris*, it took
him twenty years to find his way out of that labyrinth.

## A Continent or Another World

Whenever a writer starts talking about the novels of today,
it quickly becomes clear that the labyrinths have been
getting bigger. If in the nineteenth century they were the
size of an ambulatory mirror and later grew to that of a
house, by the end of the twentieth century they'd taken
on the dimensions of continents and planets.

As Ernesto Sábato told Orlando Barone, one of the
best literary interviewers in Argentina:

The novel is like a continent. You suddenly find your-
self crossing a swamp or a vast marshland, or traveling long roads of dirt and mud to reach a beautiful
place. I think Borges said once that he found those
dry roads boring, and that they must seem that way to
the reader, as well. But if you want to find treasure in
the Mato Grosso, you must be prepared for anything.

We finally arrive, then, at the reason certain twentieth-
century poets despised the novel: with all its hypocrisy
and cynicism, with its tendency to borrow from different
people, places, and ideas, the novel is able to create a self-
sufficient world inhabited by immortal beings. As Cyril
Connolly wrote in *Enemies of Promise*, "A great writer
creates a world and his readers are proud to live in it."

Despite its irony and misdirection, despite its imperfec-
tions, the fact that these images of the novel have survived
whispers to us that the faith great writers have in the world
of fiction has never waned. Knowing this is enough to
make you want to sit down and write.

A novel we can't make heads or tails of

# *Tool for Writing a Novel*

1. Deep down, every novel is about struggling with an obsession:

or a mystery:

2. Deep down, every novel involves a mystery someone is trying to solve: the mystery of their life, imagined or real.

3. Imagine your life as a novel, and draw its shape here:

# The Character Tree

For Ricardo Yáñez

Write your character's name.

Above them, like leaves, write their favorite words. The ones they say most often or the ones the narrator uses to describe them.

Underneath, way down as if they were roots, write the words your character never utters, the one they'll never allow themselves to speak.

Above the leaves, as if they were stars, scatter two or three words that shape their destiny.

Beneath the roots, write the big terms that have been hidden, misplaced, lost, stolen—the ones they want to get back.

A character is a tree of words. Their soul can be found in the words they say, in the words they silence or ignore; in the words they sense, and the ones spoken in their presence.

The protagonist of *The Catcher in the Rye* never says the word "adulthood," but he knows that as soon as he is no longer a minor, his country can send him to die in the war. Without mentioning the phrase at all, Salinger wrote one of the world's greatest coming-of-age novels. One of the best about the light and shadow that a single word can cast upon a life.

If we could see what they were made of, we would understand that every character is a tree under a constellation of words.

# The Myth of the Perfect Novel

When we read Kawabata's *House of the Sleeping Beauties*, Bolaño's *The Savage Detectives*, Dick's *Ubik*, Coetzee's *Disgrace*, or Castellanos Moya's *The She-Devil in the Mirror*, we get the sensation we are holding a perfect novel in our hands. I repeat: the sensation. Producing that sensation is a question of technique.

For starters, it should be said that the perfect novel is just one of the many species that make up the vast world of the novel. It is neither the best nor the worst. It would also be dishonest to take the easy way out and say that the perfect novel is one whose ending is as definitive as a landslide.

In *Aspects of the Novel*, Forster suggests that in order to appreciate a mystery, part of one's intelligence must stop to ruminate, while the rest continues on its way. Some of the most talented novelists, then, are the ones who manage to duplicate the reader and push these doubles to spread themselves throughout the book, confronting the mysteries that the narrative creates. These loose ends can't be too numerous or demand too much attention, or it will be impossible to go on reading. They need to be slight, since even a minor excess will upset a delicate balance and the book will fall to pieces. The good novelist multiplies the reader without their even noticing. Then, like a good fisherman, they slowly draw in their net. Over the course of a novel that feels perfect, the writer acts like a juggler who arrives, presents several themes, and tosses them in the air, one by one. They are suddenly obliged to play with these themes, making different patterns with them to delight the reader. The moment arrives when the reader forgets the author and sees only these figures.

Just before concluding the performance, the juggler gathers their props and, along with them, the multiplied reader. They even take a bow, and the reader applauds— partly out of obligation, thinking to themselves, "What a shame, that novel was almost flawless, but something is missing . . ." Right at that moment, the author extends their hand and the reader gets the final theme, the one that was still suspended in the air. This is usually a red ball that had disappeared from sight long before. When the reader sees it, they think: "Incredible, a perfect novel."

Those who have used this strategy did so unconsciously at first, then with a degree of calculation each time after that. It's not the kind of thing that should be overdone, though: readers can get bored of novels that are perfect but always end with the same ball.

# Bomb Theory, or
## How to End It All

It seems easy, but it's not.

Writing the final words of a novel requires a special kind of concentration. And it's always a good idea to intuit, at least, the strategy we'll use in the end.

We could choose an ending laden with irony, allusions, and intimations like in *The Charterhouse of Parma*.

Some, however, simply cut the thread of the narrative swiftly and definitively, as if they'd taken a machete to it.

Then there are the novelists who allow us to glimpse from a distance the tragic ending we already know is coming, the ones who seem to say, kindly and astutely, "Let's get out of here, there's no need to see what happens next," as Ricardo Piglia does in *Money to Burn*: "The siren faded into the distance, disappearing when the ambulance turned the corner of Herrera and the street was finally left empty."

Sometimes it seems like a character escapes from the novel and leaves the door open behind them. Aira ends *An Episode in the Life of a Landscape Painter* with a character looking at an immense, boundless landscape, just like Paul Auster does in *Moon Palace*.

Novels don't always end with a transparent word or phrase. Umberto Eco finishes off *The Name of the Rose* with a phrase in Latin; Bolaño wraps up *The Savage Detectives* with a drawing completely open to interpretation.

If the first phrase of a novel is like riling up a bull, then the last must be like the end of a bullfight.

What we can all agree on is that a weak ending leaves us cold; a long ending runs the risk of diluting its impact. The final lines must give greater meaning to what has been read in order to bring the reader's emotions to a climax. More than a cherry on top, they should be like a wave that tosses us around and deposits us on the shore.

My sense is that the best endings work like one of three kinds of bombs.

For some, the end of a novel should be definitive. It should explode with that final period, beyond which nothing should exist: the universe collapses and shuts down. This is the case in *One Hundred Years of Solitude*, *Pedro Páramo*, *Moby-Dick*, *The Murder of Roger Ackroyd*, and *The Catcher in the Rye*; when Anna Karenina throws herself onto the train tracks, or when D'Artagnan dies at the end of *Twenty Years After*. When these authors close their novels, they brick over the doorway to a vault they have no intention of ever opening again, like at the end of *Vanity Fair*, when W. M. Thackeray writes: "Ah! *Vanitas Vanitatum*! Which of us is happy in this world? Which of us has his desire? Or, having it, is satisfied? —Come, children, let us shut up the box and the puppets, for our play is played out."

Others, including the great Simon Leys in the essay cited earlier, remind us that bombs can also be set to detonate with a delay: parting words that show us the story's true conclusion little by little, seconds or minutes after we close the book.

And then there are those that work like firebombs: they don't cause a big bang on impact, but the flames burn for a long time. Sometimes until they consume the whole building.

Sardonic and cynical, the endings of Raymond Chandler's seven novels are perfect examples of explosive endings, of the mastery of a writer fully conscious of how many balls he has in the air as he approaches the final pages. In six of them, after allowing Philip Marlowe to toss out a few devastating observations about the good intentions of the other characters, after recognizing that justice will never really be done in his city, that the truth will never really be known, and that our hero is going to end up just as sad and lonely as when the adventure began, Marlowe's perfect words reveal what remains of the main players after their harrowing experiences:

And in a little while he too, like Rusty Regan, would be sleeping the big sleep. On the way downtown I stopped at a bar and had a couple of double Scotches. They didn't do me any good. All they did was make me think of Silver-Wig, and I never saw her again. (*The Big Sleep*)

It was a cool day and very clear. You could see a long way—but not as far as Velma had gone. (*Farewell, My Lovely*)

Then I carried my glass out to the kitchen, rinsed it and filled it with ice water, and stood at the sink sipping it and looking at my face in the mirror.
    "You and Capablanca," I said. (*The High Window*)

Something that had been a man. (*The Lady in the Lake*)

"I guess somebody lost a dream," the intern said. He bent over and closed her eyes. (*The Little Sister*)

I never saw any of them again—except the cops. No way has yet been invented to say goodbye to them. (*The Long Goodbye*)

When you read an ending as perfect as these, you want to start the whole book over again to get a better look at the hammer that drives these nails so well.

The power of Chandler's endings, the elegant way they examine what remains after the battle, seems to have made an impression on many of the authors of detective fiction that followed. Just take a look at the endings of Leonardo Sciascia, Henning Mankell, James Ellroy: the detectives in their novels reach the final pages spent and exhausted, like shipwrecked sailors dragging themselves onto the sand.

The novels that resolve like timebombs include those with open or ambiguous endings, which may take us days— or years—to decipher. I'm thinking about the final words of *The Sheltering Sky* by Paul Bowles, after which you can't say for sure what will happen to the protagonist when she stops her vehicle; about which conclusion in Ágota Kristóf's Notebook Trilogy is the real one; about the wanderings of the protagonists in Cormac McCarthy's *All the Pretty Horses* and Bohumil Hrabal's *I Served the King of England*.

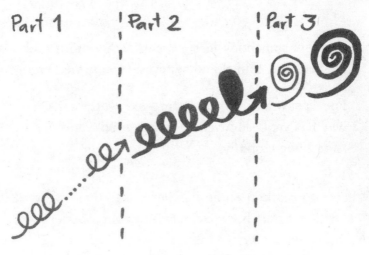

*The Notebook Trilogy* by Ágota Kristóf

The fact is, as the author reaches the end of a novel, they need to gather as many of their characters as possible before they lift their pen that last time. For the reader who has been carried along by the passions and violence in play, that final phrase should be as intense as someone's dying words.

In *Severina*, Rodrigo Rey Rosa pulls off one of the greatest firebomb endings I know. Parting words that might seem cryptic to someone who hasn't read the rest of the novel, but when we know the characters and the story, and hear these final lines, we feel as if someone just set our clothes ablaze: "And maybe one day Severina will tear out some of her hair and scatter it over my body." Part of the strategy employed by these fiery endings, from *Don Quixote* to *The Murder of Roger Ackroyd*, rests on the fact that these authors withhold the surprising transformation of their characters until the last moment, as if it were an ace up their sleeve.

*No Sacred Place* by Rodrigo Rey Rosa

James Cain's superbly bitter novel *The Postman Always Rings Twice*, which Jorge Luis Borges and Adolfo Bioy Casares published in their legendary collection, "The Seventh Circle," ends with three extraordinary pages, in which one of the two protagonists is sentenced to death. When he learns he has only moments to live, he entreats the reader: "Here they come. Father McConnell says prayers help. If you've got this far, send one up for me, and Cora, and make it that we're together, wherever it is." In these three pages, a character who has surprised and terrified us with his cold-blooded cynicism experiences one last, indisputable twist of fate and realizes that he's reached the end of the road. He looks back on the decisions that got him where he is, passes judgment on his life, and begs for our understanding in a final phrase that is so extraordinary because it is so unexpected, because it reveals a greater depth to the character than we'd expected. This kind of ending can be found, of course, in condensed form in Borges's story "The Garden of Forking Paths," when the protagonist, after confessing his crime, issues a plea to the reader ... and also in *The Invention of Morel* by Bioy Casares, when a man begs the reader to unite him with the woman he loves, and to believe, as he does, that such a thing is possible.

*The Invention of Morel* by Adolfo Bioy Casares

Without saying anything directly, the end of *The Old Man
and the Sea* suggests an extraordinary conclusion, a long-
deserved reward: Hemingway writes in the final lines of
his magnificent short novel that the old man dreams of
lions. For someone who hasn't read the novel, this ending might seem enigmatic; for those just finishing it, these
final words will stir their emotions and echo inside them.

Reading a good novel is like spending time with people
able to change our point of view. That's why we feel such
a deep sadness when we reach the end of one. That voice
we've had with us for so long . . . Will we ever hear it
again? How did we get so attached to a being made only
of words?

Is this why we're so glad to see a character again, even
if they die in another novel? Why we jump for joy to see
Captain Nemo in *In Search of the Castaways*, the three
musketeers in *Twenty Years After*, Tomáš and Tereza in the
epilogue to *The Unbearable Lightness of Being*, Sherlock
Holmes in a story after the one where he fell off a cliff
while fighting Moriarty, Kurt Wallander or the detective of
our choice in their next adventure? Perhaps so. Perhaps it
is because, with this surprising gesture, the novel whispers
to us that even if these stories seem to reach a definitive
end, life goes on in other ways.

# What Lives at the Bottom
# of the Lagoon

For Julio Villanueva Chang

Sometimes it isn't effort, but chance, which provides the key element that gives us the face of a carefully considered novel. This is often the case with titles, though even the first sentence of a story, that magnet that draws the reader in, might be dictated by happenstance.

Following a tradition that seems to come from the Middle Ages, some choose a title that matches the first words of their story, when those opening words announce something extraordinary: *If on a Winter's Night a Traveler*, *Pereira Declares* ...

Others name their novels after their protagonists, confident that we will become their accomplices as soon as we read their stories: *Anna Karenina, Madame Bovary, Tom Sawyer, Huckleberry Finn, Gulliver's Travels, Oedipus Rex, Macbeth, King Lear, Don Quixote, Gargantua and Pantagruel, Tristram Shandy, Moby-Dick, Pedro Páramo, Ulysses, The Brothers Karamazov, Nadja, The Death of*

*Artemio Cruz, Galaor, Adriana Buenos Aires, Père Goriot, Oryx and Crake.*

Still others choose a word of particular importance to their protagonist as their title: *Money, Shame, Submission, Serotonin, Silk, Amber, Zombie, Blonde, Indignation, Little Eyes, Jazz, Paradise, Home, Timbuktu, The Pearl, The Stranger, The Plague, Homegoing, The Gambler, Demons, The Shining, The Rehearsal.* Sometimes the title is an unknown word that takes on unexpected meaning as we read: *Herzog, Ubik, Sula, Limonov, Dracula, Frankenstein, The Hobbit.*

Sometimes a title will consist of two words with obvious symbolic weight, joined together for a mysterious reason: *The Red and the Black, Crime and Punishment, War and Peace, The Prince and the Pauper, Pride and Prejudice, The Sound and the Fury, The Old Man and the Sea, Fear and Trembling, The Master and Margarita.* These two words can be combined in infinite ways: *News from the Empire, Kingdom Cons, The Music of Chance, The Buddha of Suburbia, A Wizard of Earthsea, The Sorrows of an American, To Kill a Mockingbird, The Gravedigger's Daughter, The Volcano Lover, Strangers on a Train, The Catcher in the Rye, The Ages of Lulu, A Confederacy of Dunces.*

The stroke of genius might also be found in an adjective: *The Blind Assassin, The Satanic Verses, The Mysterious Island, The Glass Key, The Maltese Falcon, Red Harvest, The Long Goodbye, The Big Sleep, The Martian*

*Chronicles, The Last Reader, The Wild Palms, Dead Souls, American Gods, The Lean Lands, Small Lives, The Magic Mountain, The Dying Animal, Invisible Cities, My Brilliant Friend.*

Some titles act as a debriefing after an extraordinary experience: *How I Became a Nun, The Metamorphosis, Ilona Arrives with the Rain, A Connecticut Yankee in King Arthur's Court, Journey to the End of the Night, Dark as the Grave Wherein My Friend Is Laid, Twenty Thousand Leagues under the Sea, From the Earth to the Moon, In the Country of Last Things, A Pale View of Hills, An Artist of the Floating World, In Search of Lost Time, The Unbearable Lightness of Being, The Name of the Rose, The Invention of Morel, The Plain in Flames, Where the Air Is Clear, London after Midnight, Deep Waters, Accordion Crimes, A Heart So White, Tomorrow in the Battle Think on Me, The She-Devil in the Mirror, The Private Lives of Trees, The Long Night of White Chickens, The Brief Wondrous Life of Oscar Wao, A History of the World in 10½ Chapters, Memories of the Future, Light in August.*

Others have the force of an aphorism or a revelation: *The Heart Is a Lonely Hunter, The Postman Always Rings Twice, I Married a Communist, Let's Go with Pancho Villa, The Great Swindle, The Left Hand of Darkness, Dark Back of Time, No Country for Old Men, Oblivion: A Memoir, Vast Emotions and Imperfect Thoughts, Life Is Elsewhere.*

Some writers prefer titles that take up a few lines and hint at the story's opening. They invite us to wonder *For Whom the Bell Tolls*, whether it's true that *The Postman Always Rings Twice*, exactly how *I Served the King of England*, what happened in that *Episode in the Life of a Landscape Painter*, who was *The Man Who Loved Dogs*, what were the details of *The Incredible and Sad Tale of Innocent Eréndira and Her Heartless Grandmother* and the *Chronicle of a Death Foretold*, what kind of person would proclaim *I'd Receive the Worst News from Your Beautiful Lips*, or what might make us exclaim *Because It Seems like a Lie the Truth Is Never Known*. Then, of course, there's *The Story of a Shipwrecked Sailor Who Drifted on a Life Raft for Ten Days without Food or Water, Was Proclaimed a National Hero, Kissed by Beauty Queens and Made Wealthy by Publicity, and Then Spurned by the Government and Forgotten for All Time*. Worthy of special mention is the recent wave of excellent Nordic fiction with titles that feature a woman or a man, or sometimes both: *The Girl Who Played with Fire*, *The Girl with the Dragon Tattoo*, *The Hundred-Year-Old Man Who Climbed Out the Window and Disappeared*, *The Girl Who Saved the King of Sweden*. If we applied this logic to our own classics (and why not?) we'd get: *The Man Who Pursued a White Whale and Went Down with His Ship*, *The Tyrant Who Ruled a Town of the Dead*, *The Vampire Who Went to London for a Meal and Met His Destiny*.

These are all the product of a healthy dose of effort, but titles don't only come from careful thought during the time we spend with our eyes open. Chance does its own writing, too. A brief note beside a painting in New York's MoMA reminds us that in 1927, the painter Yves Tanguy asked André Breton for help with the titles of the canvasses that would appear in his first gallery show in Paris. Tanguy, who felt more comfortable painting his pieces than trying to describe them, was worried about finding words to match the content of his paintings—which were part underwater landscape and part portrait of the end of the world—and had generally limited himself to numbering or dating them. That's where Breton came in. But the gallery opening was swiftly approaching, and the poet was nowhere to be found. The day finally arrived and Tanguy had two dozen impressive canvasses without titles. The gallerist demanded he differentiate them somehow, to avoid confusion, so Tanguy left the gallery just a few hours before it opened and went to find Breton where he was staying—probably at the Hôtel des Grands Hommes. The surrealist got up from his desk, put on a blazer, and, just as they were about to leave for the gallery, grabbed a book: Nobel laureate Charles Richet's *Treatise on Metaphysics*. Tanguy, on the verge of a nervous breakdown, wondered how the leader of the surrealist movement was going to come up with the right names for his complex paintings in so little time. Breton walked around the gallery, more excited by the minute; when he'd seen the whole exhibition, he opened the book on metaphysics at random and chose the phrases he thought best suited the works. To Tanguy's surprise, these all managed to amplify the meaning of his canvasses, as if placing them on a pedestal. And this is how the fabulous, disconcerting paintings of Tanguy's first solo show got the titles that have made their way into history: *Extinction of Useless Lights*, *He Did What He Wanted*, and *Mama, Papa Is Wounded!*

By combining chance with scientific precision, the poetic genius of Breton gave names to images that seem to float in the air and, in so doing, multiplied the profound sense of strangeness we get when we look at Tanguy's paintings: part underwater dusk, part dreamscape inhabited by objects we've never seen before and may never see again.

# Once upon a Time

For Marçel Aquino

When you think you've lost your way in the story you're writing; when your language and your technique seem to obscure what you're trying to say; whenever you suspect that there's too little or too much of something in your story but don't know what it is, or you find that your novel has branched off in so many directions that you can't find the center anymore, there are two ways to get your bearings.

If you prefer the daylight path, ask your protagonist what they want and why they want it so badly, where they are when their story begins and ends. That way, you can see them at the highest points in their journey and determine how urgently they are trying to achieve their goals. You'll have to stretch a tightrope between these two points for your hero to cross.

But you can also take the nocturnal path, the path of magic, of the circus performer who soars through the air without a net. It's a far riskier path, and it means invoking forces as ancient as the origins of literature itself. If you're willing to take that risk, if you're willing to bet it all on a single hand, instead of asking your hero what they want, say out loud these four words that will make you begin the whole story over again, dispensing with the superfluous and starting fresh from this new threshold. If one day you think nothing is working and you have no idea where you're headed, just say the words "Once upon a time . . ." and begin the story you're trying to write again from that initial phrase. You'll be surprised what you're capable of, using that improvisation. You'll see how the hollow elements of your story shrink to the point of disappearing, and how the more promising ones demand room to grow. Whole chapters will disappear as if by magic, and traits that only barely appeared in your characters will take on enormous weight, becoming absolutely central. Meanwhile, the chain of cause and effect emerges clearly before our eyes, and we see which elements there still need work: which of its links make the story more (or less) interesting, which represent surprising twists of fate, which test the will of our heroes, which allow our narrator to witness everything and tell us where it's all headed.

In the first case, you're trying to discover where your hero wants to go and where their adventure will lead them, like a film producer; in the second, you're trying to understand which elements make the story interesting and worthy of being told until the end of days, as is the dream of all fabulists.

Why does this work? Because if we do it well, it reminds us how important it is to be told stories as night falls, how much we need them to explain the moment we find ourselves in, and how necessary it is for all storytellers, across the ages, to keep wanting to find new ways to say "Once upon a time" in their own words, and to keep telling the same story about humanity, each with their own voice.

# My Uncle and the Tiger

For Victor Del Árbol

It was more than six feet long, from its head to the tip of its tail. When we went to visit, my sisters, cousins, and I would lie on the enormous monster; we would jump and roll all over it and then suddenly two or more of us would get under its skin, lift it up, and chase after the others. When we calmed down again, we would ask my uncle how the animal's back came to have those two big holes with burnt edges in it, and my uncle would tell us the best story of his entire life.

The tiger had attacked my uncle one night, and my uncle Jesús had killed it in self-defense. He'd decided not long before that he wanted to live in the country, so he dragged his wife and children to a place far from any major thoroughfare where they lived through two cyclones, as many tropical storms as a Caribbean island sees in August, and as many surprises as anyone living at the base of a mountain is likely to get.

One of these surprises was the tiger. Not long after moving in, and against every piece of advice he'd been given, my uncle bought three expensive cows, a foreign breed never before seen in the area, and set all his hopes on them. When the oldest ranch hands saw them, they all said the same thing: "We've never had that kind of animal around here, who knows what'll come of it." Not long after, one of the cows disappeared, and my uncle and a ranch hand spent two days looking for it, with no luck. Then they saw vultures circling in the sky. They headed toward the base of the mountain, and just as they were about to give up, the ranch hand pointed to large spots of blood on the fallen leaves. The buzzing of flies caught their attention, and they looked up to find the cow's remains hanging from a high branch on one of the tallest ceibas around. When my uncle asked how the hell his cow had climbed the tree, or what scoundrel had stuck her up there, the ranch hand shook his head and explained that when there was no food on the mountainside, the bigger predators would come down and hunt the livestock. And that the only one of those animals that could grip a cow in its jaws and leap into the branches of a tree like that was the fanged beast people around there called tigers, but which were actually jaguars, because there were no tigers in that part of the world. The animal that ate his cow wasn't striped; its coat was marked by a constellation of dark, round spots, those "incorruptible and eternal forms," as Borges described them in "The Writing of the God."

A month later, they found the bones of a bigger cow under an ominous flock of vultures. The same discovery was repeated several weeks later, with the third cow. By that time, the ranch hands had told my uncle that the beast had gotten a taste for his cows and that nothing would prevent it from attacking them when they went home at night, cutting their way through the jungle with their machetes, or, God forbid, from attacking the children when they went outside to play. The only way to avoid a tragedy was to hunt the animal down. My uncle Jesús says that from that moment on, he forbade my cousins to venture far from the house and ordered the few ranch hands who had rifles to stand guard over the rest of the cattle. Contrary to his initial practice of letting his animals roam free, he began corralling them. Crisis was averted for a while, but everyone knew that the animal was still there, lurking in the dark.

The end of the month arrived, bringing with it the obligation to pay the ranch hands. My uncle set out for the city early in the morning to withdraw money from the bank, but the roads were so narrow and travel was so difficult in the mountains that night surprised him on the way back, just as he was reaching the stables. When they reached a place where the path disappeared in the underbrush, his horse reared and tried so hard to turn around that my uncle struggled to regain control. The hair on the back of his neck stood up when he realized that the animal wasn't crazy, it was terrified. My uncle held the reins tight, and his horse spun two or three times in place; because he was carrying his lantern, he saw the two huge emerald-green eyes glint just a few steps from his horse. He fumbled his rifle out of its holster and fired until there were no bullets left. The ranch hands who ran to his aid helped him find, not far from there, a great beast like the ones in novels by B. Traven that grab donkeys in their maws and leap up into the treetops to devour them. The next day, my uncle headed to the news office closest to him looking for a photographer. It took two mules to hoist the tiger up by braided ropes tied to its torso so that my uncle, who was young and thin back then, could pose beside it with the eyeglasses he wore for nearsightedness and his diminutive rifle. The photographer liked the portrait so much that he sent it to all the local papers.

My grandmother, who lived in Mexico City, learned of the whole episode when she turned on a national news broadcast and the most popular anchor on television concluded with a stranger-than-fiction true story: "Some people travel to Africa to hunt tigers, for pleasure, but Mr. Jesús Heredia hunts them in self-defense on the doorstep of his own home." And there was the photo of my uncle posing in his bookish eyeglasses next to a monster much bigger and broader than him. My grandmother, who was financing my uncle's foray into ranching and had believed that he was living in an idyll where he was never in any danger, hopped on the first plane to Tampico and from there got on the highway, determined to give her firstborn a piece of her mind and demand that he return to the city. Before he did, my uncle had the tiger skinned by an artisan who reconstructed the animal's head and added a row of sharp fangs, all authentic. And that was how the hide and the photo of the tiger reached the living room of this house.

Many years after my uncle Jesús died, I was chatting with my aunt Carmen and asked her to tell me the story of the tiger. I told her my version and she sighed. "Ay, mijito," she said tenderly. "That's how your uncle told it, but that's not how it was at all." And she made three corrections.

First: It was the head rancher who killed the tiger, not my uncle Jesús. During the attack my uncle barely managed to control his horse, which had gone wild with fear. It was the head rancher, who was traveling with him and who'd spent his whole life breaking horses, who managed to draw his rifle as the tiger was about to pounce and fire it until he ran out of bullets. He did all this before his horse's front hooves returned to the ground.

Second: The tiger didn't die right away; it managed to escape. The real adventure was much more complicated than the story, because it involved convincing a group of terrified ranch hands that it was absolutely necessary to track an injured beast through the night and kill it under the light of the Gulf sky. Otherwise, as the eldest among them pointed out, the people and animals on all the surrounding ranches were in grave danger: a tiger, when wounded, becomes a raging killer. They found it dying but still capable of impressive feats in a cave at the base of the mountain. The tiger tried to escape when they surrounded it, leaping from side to side, but the shooters hit their mark. Its chest was still moving, though, as it dragged itself across the ground, so the group needed to fire one more time, for something the ranch hands called mercy.

Third: It was my uncle who took this last shot, but not because he was brave. His neighbors forced him to do it. "This is your fault," they said. "You started all this when you brought in your strange cows, so now you need to finish it." And that was how a very nearsighted young man came to straighten his glasses and face down the greatest fear he'd ever known.

I jumped up to look again at the photograph that my cousins loved so much. I wanted the whole truth, so we took it down from where it hung on the living room wall and removed it from its frame. For the first time in my life, I noticed that it had been folded. The most memorable short stories need that fold in order to work. The original image contained not only the imposing ceiba, the monstrous tiger hanging from it by thick ropes, and the bespectacled hunter posing beside the animal's remains. It also revealed a third character, a few steps away, who appeared when the picture was unfolded: a short, muscular Indigenous man in a plaid shirt and cowboy boots, holding the reins of the mules that had pulled the beast upright.

A man and a tiger are all it takes to tell a story about life and death. But if what we want is a novel, we have to take the photograph out of its frame, unfold it, and ask ourselves where the truth lies: who killed the tiger, and whose hands are around the ropes that hold up the world.

# A Timeline of the Novel,
# 8th century BCE to Now

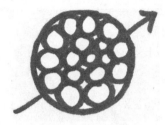

*The Life before Us* by Émile Ajar

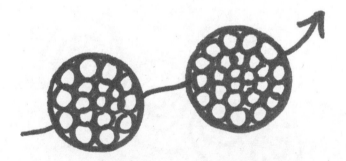

*Beloved* by Toni Morrison

*The Wind-Up Bird Chronicle* by Haruki Murakami

*Oryx and Crake* (left) and *The Handmaid's Tale* (right)
by Margaret Atwood

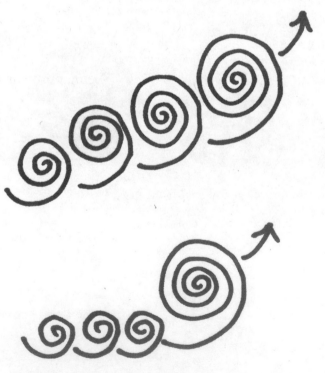

*Hurricane Season* (top) and *Paradais* (bottom)
by Fernanda Melchor

# Acknowledgments

For Vesta,
Mateo, Mariana, and Joaquín,
with novelesque joy;

To the memory of Martín Solares Téllez
and Rogelio Amor Tejada;

And to the following people—please match your name
to one or more of these reasons:

My mother, Rosario Heredia — with love

Gely and Taty

Mónica Cuevas — in gratitude

Ignacio Herrerías Cuevas
and Ignacio Herrerías Montoya — for their Quixotic
friendship

The family of Barragán Heredia

The Paris group

Doctor Avelino Gaitán
and Paloma Villegas,
especially — for their unblemished
friendship in this
sublunar world

Marcos Eymar                          for their advice
Freddy Domínguez
Augusto Cruz
Francisco Barrenechea
Rubén Gallo                           for their literary
Hervé Le Corré                        complicity
Karim Benmiloud
Claude Fell
Christilla Vasserot                   for their solidarity with
Dominique Bourgois                    my book
Florence Olivier
Jorge Volpi
Eduardo Antonio Parra                 for drawing their
Sergio Pitol                          novels
Diana Carolina Rey
Héctor Abad Faciolince
Danilo Moreno
Pietro and Maddalena Torrigiani
Malaspina                             for reading this manu-
Ricardo Yáñez                         script with novelesque
Marcelo Uribe                         passion
Francisco Hinojosa
Siri Hustvedt & Paul Auster
Miguel Syjuco
Junot Díaz                            for their generosity
Francisco Goldman                     with extravagant ideas
Manuel Monroy

Hugo Hiriart & Guita Schyfter         for trying to convince
Quino and Alicia                      me to stop drawing and
                                      get back to writing

# Notes

p 9 **she was a tarantula:** Alejandro Jodorowsky, *The Dance of Reality* (trans. Ariel Godwin), 70–72.

p 12 **been searching in vain:** Constantin Stanislawski, *La construction du personage* (Paris: Pygmalion, 2006), 28.

p 20 **about myself is necessary:** Ernesto Sábato, *The Tunnel* (trans. Margaret Sayers Peden); **road in northern Wisconsin:** These lines come from *Moon Palace*, *The Brooklyn Follies*, and *Leviathan*, respectively; **botfly is still there:** Mario Vargas Llosa, *The War of the End of the World* (trans. Helen Lane), and *The Green House* (trans. Gregory Rabassa).

p 33 **world around you fade:** Or, like Michel Butor in *Second Thoughts*: "Standing with your left foot on the grooved brass sill, you try in vain with your right shoulder to push the sliding door a little wider open. You edge your way in through the narrow opening."

p 36 **first and last lines:** Louis Aragon, *Je n'ai jamais appris à écrire ou les Incipit* (Paris: Flammarion, 1981), 93.

p 40 **common to all the arts:** *Andrei Tarkovsky, Le temps scellé* (Paris: Petite Bibliothèque des Cahiers du Cinéma, 1989), 75.

p 53 **that we have gone:** "Things" (trans. Stephen Kessler), in *Borges: Selected Poems.*

p 112 **written despite its author:** Juan José Arreola, "Memoria y olvido," in *La ficción de la memoria: Juan Rulfo ante la crítica* (Mexico City: Ediciones Era, 2003), 504; **Faulkner, Proust, and Joyce:** Mariana Frenk, "Pedro Páramo," in *La ficción de la memoria,* 45–46; **we have from Sophocles:** Gabriel García Márquez, "Breves nostalgias sobre Juan Rulfo," in *La ficción de la memoria,* 453.

p 113 **come to us in dreams:** For more on this subject, see Fabienne Bradu's fine book *Ecos de Páramo* (Mexico City: Fondo de Cultural Económica, 1989) and Jorge Aguilar Mora's essay "Las piedras de Juan Rulfo," in *La ficción de la memoria;* **the dust, the pirú:** Octavio Paz, "Paisaje y novela en México" (The landscape and the novel in Mexico), in *Corriente alterna* (Mexico City: Siglo XXI, 1971), 18. TN: The pirú (*Schinus molle*) is a tree with a thick trunk and reddish bark that can grow up to forty feet.

p 114 **never say how they think:** Margo Glantz, "Juan Rulfo: la forma de la muerte," in *La ficción de la memoria,* 376–67; **they really are ghosts:** Augusto Monterroso, "Los fantasmas de Rulfo," in *La vaca* (Mexico City: Alfaguara, 2003).

p 115 **moments of grief or cruelty:** Felipe Garrido, quoted by Jorge Ruffinelli in *La ficción de la memoria,* 330–31. For more on Rulfo's humor, I recommend reading the essays by Antonio Alatorre, Felipe Garrido, and Ruffinnelli in that same volume; **to the Media Luna:** TN: The Media Luna (Half Moon) is the name of Pedro Páramo's land.

p 116 **sides of the same coin:** Emir Rodríguez Monegal, "Relectura de *Pedro Páramo*," in *La ficcion de la memoria*, 132; **lighting it up at night:** Rulfo, *Pedro Páramo* (trans. Douglas J. Weatherford), 2; **a cause for shame:** Bradu, *Ecos de Páramo*.

p 119 **Polish reporters bothering him:** These articles can be found, respectively, in *La ficción de la memoria*: Benítez, "Conversaciones con Juan Rulfo," 548; Elena Poniatowska, "¡Ay, vida, no me mereces!" 526; and Felipe Cobián, "Los pueblos de Rulfo," 462–63.

p 122 **him, a very bad one:** Roberto García Bonilla, "Juan Rulfo y la Ciudad de México" in *La ficción de la memoria*, 389.

p 123 **the capo from Tuxcacuesco:** In the first version of the novel, which is discussed in *Cuadernos de Juan Rulfo* (ed. Yvette Jiménez de Báez), Abundio the mule driver is killed "during the revolution," but this information does not appear in the final version. Rulfo cut the historical reference so readers could remain focused on their surprise at the possibility that Abundio, whom they had just seen moments earlier, might be dead.

p 124 **events of his life:** Joseph Sommers, "Los muertos no tienen tiempo ni espacio," in *La ficción de la memoria*, 519; **want to help them:** Manuel Durán, "Juan Rulfo, cuentista: la verdad casi sospechosa," in *La ficción de la memoria*, 98.

p 125 **an unrelenting senile passion:** Respectively, Sommers, "Los muertos," 519; Blanco Aguinaga, "Realidad y estilo de Juan Rulfo," 32; and García Márquez, "Breves nostalgias," 453, in *La ficción de la memoria*.

p 126 **doing it for him:** Aguinaga in *La ficción de la memoria*, 30; **his imagined characters did:** Sommers, "Los muertos," in *La ficción de la memoria*, 519; **and, consequently, a lie:** Benítez, "Conversaciones con Juan Rulfo," in *La ficción de la memoria*, 547; **the entirety of a human life:** José Emilio Pacheco, "Juan Rulfo en 1959," in *La ficción de la memoria*, 446; **essential to the work:** García Bonilla, "Juan Rulfo y la Ciudad," in *La ficción de la memoria*, 382.

p 127 **the impact of death:** Glantz, "Juan Rulfo: la forma de la muerte," in *La ficción de la memoria*, 370; **the way people talk:** Luis Harss, "Juan Rulfo o la pena sin nombre," in *La ficción de la memoria*, 87.

p 128 **of an imagined being:** Juan Villoro, "Lección de arena" in *Efectos personales* (Mexico City: Ediciones Era, 2000), 16.

p 129 **here in the ground:** Rulfo, *Pedro Páramo*, 60.

p 130 **the realm of ambiguity:** In his interview with José Carlos González Boixo, the Jaliscan writer acknowledged that the characters in his novel often enter the territory of imagination: the incestuous siblings are no more than a hallucination of Juan Preciado; Susana misses the sea without ever having seen it and talks to a lover who never existed. In *Cuadernos de Juan Rulfo*, Rulfo states that the novel is "a world in which fantasy is sometimes mistaken for reality" (169).

p. 133 *La pensée du roman* (2003); revised and translated into English as *The Lives of the Novel* (Princeton, NJ: Princeton University Press, 2013).

p 145 **puddles at your feet:** Stendhal, *The Red and the Black*, *vol.* 2, ch. 19; **jump into the mirror:** Jean-Paul Sartre, *Situations I*, 14, quoted in Alain Rey, *Dictionnaire culturel en langue française* (Paris: Le Robert, 2005), 655.

p 147 **to cut at all:** André Gide, *The Counterfeiters*, trans. Dorothy Bussy (New York: Vintage, 1973), 187.

p 150 **other book-tremulation can do:** D. H. Lawrence, *Study of Thomas Hardy and Other Essays*, 195.

p 153 **be prepared for anything:** Orlando Barone, *Diálogos Borges-Sábato* (Buenos Aires: Emecé, 1976), 50–51.

# Selected Bibliography

Arenas, Reinaldo. *Hallucinations: Or, the Ill-Fated Peregrinations of Fray Servando* (trans. Andrew Hurley). New York: Penguin Books, 2002.

Atxaga, Bernardo. *The Lone Man* (trans. Margaret Jull Costa). London: Harvill, 1996.

Bioy Casares, Adolfo. *The Invention of Morel* (trans. Ruth L. C. Simms). New York: NYRB Classics, 2003.

Bolaño, Roberto. *2666* (trans. Natasha Wimmer). New York: Farrar, Straus & Giroux, 2008.

Borges, Jorge Luis. *Borges: Selected Poems* (ed. Alexander Coleman). New York: Penguin Books, 2000.

Cabrera Infante, Guillermo. *Three Trapped Tigers* (trans. Suzanne Jill Levine). New York: Harper & Row, 1978.

Capote, Truman. *In Cold Blood*. New York: Vintage, 1965.

Castellanos Moya, Horacio. *The She-Devil in the Mirror* (trans. Katherine Silver). New York: New Directions, 2009.

———. *Revulsion: Thomas Bernhard in San Salvador* (trans. Lee Klein). New York: New Directions, 2016.

Dürrenmatt, Friedrich. *The Judge and His Hangman*, in *The Inspector Barlach Mysteries* (trans. Joel Agee). Chicago: University of Chicago Press, 2006.

Echenoz, Jean. *I'm Gone* (trans. Mark Polizotti). New York: New Press, 2014.

Eco, Umberto. *The Name of the Rose* (trans. William Weaver). New York: Harcourt Brace, 1983.

García Márquez, Gabriel. *The Autumn of the Patriarch* (trans. Gregory Rabassa). New York: Harper & Row, 1976.

————. *Chronicle of a Death Foretold* (trans. Gregory Rabassa). New York: Alfred A. Knopf, 1983.

————. *The Story of a Shipwrecked Sailor* (trans. Randolph Hogan). New York: Alfred A. Knopf, 1986.

Gombrowicz, Witold. *Ferdydurke* (trans. Eric Mosbacher). New York: Grove Press, 1967.

Highsmith, Patricia. *Deep Water.* New York: Norton, 1957.

Ibargüengoitia, Jorge. *The Lightning of August* (trans. Irene del Corral). New York: Avon Books, 1986.

Jodorowsky, Alejandro. *The Dance of Reality* (trans. Ariel Godwin). Rochester, VT: Park Street Press, 2014.

Lowry, Malcolm. *Under the Volcano.* New York: Reynal & Hitchcock, 1947.

Márai, Sándor. *Embers* (trans. Carol Brown Janeway). New York: Alfred A. Knopf, 2001.

Marías, Javier. *Tomorrow in the Battle Think on Me* (trans. Margaret Jull Costa). New York: New Directions, 2001.

Musil, Robert. *The Man without Qualities* (trans. Eithne Wilkins and Ernst Kaiser). New York: Capricorn Books, 1965.

Mutis, Álvaro. *The Tramp Steamer's Last Port of Call*, in *The Adventures of Maqroll* (trans. Edith Grossman). New York: Harper Collins, 1995.

Onetti, Juan Carlos. *Goodbyes and Stories* (trans. Daniel Balderston). Austin: University of Texas Press, 1990.

Rey Rosa, Rodrigo. *Severina* (trans. Chris Andrews). New Haven: Yale University Press, 2014.

Roncagliolo, Santiago. *Red April* (trans. Edith Grossman). New York: Pantheon, 2009.

Rulfo, Juan. *Pedro Páramo* (trans. Douglas J. Weatherford). New York: Grove Press, 2023.

Sábato, Ernesto. *The Tunnel* (trans. Margaret Sayers Peden). New York: Penguin, 2011.

Seger, Linda. *Advanced Screenwriting*. Los Angeles: Silman-James Press, 2003.

Stendhal. *The Charterhouse of Parma* (trans. C. K. Scott Moncrieff). New York: Liveright, 1944.

Vargas Llosa, Mario. *The Green House* (trans. Gregory Rabassa). New York: Harper & Row, 1968.

———. *The War of the End of the World* (trans. Helen R. Lane). London: Faber and Faber, 1986.

———. *Who Killed Palomino Molero?* (trans. Alfred Mac-Adam). New York: Noonday Press, 1998.

———. *The Feast of the Goat* (trans. Edith Grossman). New York: Picador, 2002.

Vila-Matas, Enrique. *Never Any End to Paris* (trans. Anne MacLean). New York: New Directions, 2011.

Zambra, Alejandro. *Bonsai* (trans. Carolina de Robertis). New York: Melville House, 2008.

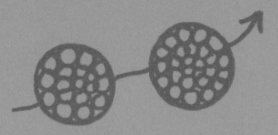

*BELOVED* BY TONI MORRISON

*ORLANDO* BY VIRGINIA WOOLF

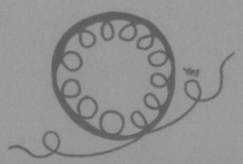

Yes

*ULYSSES* BY JAMES JOYCE